Beer: A Memoir

JAMES KIRKHAM

ISBN-13: 978-1541340992

For Dad
Miss you

1 INTRODUCTION

'Beer is Great' claimed the t-shirts being sold at the time. They were right. Although I was only just starting to realise it when the t-shirts were for sale in the late 1980s, it didn't take me long to discover that beer really was great. Thirty years later and my view is still the same. Beer might be very different, but it is still great.

The t-shirts were being sold by the enormously successful *Viz* comic (or was it a magazine?) which at the time was selling around a million copies per issue. It doesn't sell anywhere near that now. It is still going, although it has been pushed further up newsagents' shelves in an increasingly Puritan age. It now sits alongside the plastic wrapped *Readers' Wives* and *Asian Babes*. The range of merchandise has expanded and many of the old t-shirt designs have remained, proudly extolling the virtues of things like cigarettes, lard and fighting. When I discovered it, *Viz* was at the height of its commercial and creative powers in an age before rampant political correctness. It was full of outlandish characters with more than a fair share of anarchy and offensiveness. Regular characters like *Sid the Sexist*, *Biffa Bacon* and *The Fat Slags* as well as the genius *Top Tips* and *Letters* pages were laugh out loud funny.

I had been raised on comics as a child and one was delivered each week with the morning paper. I'd started with *Beano* and *Whizzer and Chips* before moving onto war comics like *Commando* and *Victor* as well as a spell with the re-launched *Eagle* after reading some of my father's originals from the late 1950s. After a spell reading magazines like *White Dwarf* and *Imagine* in my mid-teens, discovering *Viz* was a revelation. It was so funny and very, very rude. It was 1989 and in the sixth form common room at school in Halifax, it was essential reading and received far more attention than the far less amusing 'A' level texts that I should have been reading.

Besides smutty comics, there was also another much bigger distraction in that final year at school, one that continues to this day. It was in that final year at school that we discovered that, just like the t-shirt said, beer was indeed great.

I haven't bought *Viz* for many years and for a while I hadn't even realised that it was still being produced. I prefer to remember it's glory years and I still flick regularly through the compilation books with titles like *The Big Pink Stiff One*. The arrival of social media reignited my interest and I have an occasional chuckle to myself when I get an update, the *Top Tips* and *Letters* still frequently containing some modern comedic gems.

The comic itself looks relatively unchanged with lots of new characters and there is still lots of original design merchandise being sold. A picture of the *Beer is Great* popped up one day on my phone and it got me thinking. I was already wandering down memory lane because at the time I was getting rid of my bulky and increasingly tatty photograph albums and I was patiently scanning the nearly four thousand photos I had taken before finally entering the digital photography age in 2004.

Many of these photos, especially those from the early 1990s, were taken in pubs or involved beer because it was on those occasions that the camera frequently came out to capture good times, at least until the twenty-four frames had been used up. As well as the photos, there were other mementos from the period including a front page headline from *The Times* that I had saved because of its humorous (to me at least) angle and its particularly beery relevance.

So, a beery t-shirt, beery photos and a beery newspaper headline got me thinking about beer. They got me thinking about just how much things had changed since those first pints many years ago, changes which had passed me by with student and working life. It wasn't until I thought about it that I appreciated how different things were from those innocent early days in Halifax.

Also around the same time I was reading *The Times'* restaurant critic Giles Coren's book *How to Eat Out* about his time working in, eating in and writing about restaurants. It is an enormously enjoyable book which I read poolside in Las Vegas in 2013. Enjoying the book and emboldened by some terrific American 'craft' (yawn) beers in the afternoon, the combination of relaxing, sunshine and strong hoppy beer resulted in me deciding that I could *easily* write a book like that, but instead I would write one about beer.

I thought it would be easy to do. With no previous writing experience, this showed my utter naivety about taking on such a project. Little did I appreciate just how much time, effort and frustration was involved in writing a book. It has taken over four years of bursts of productivity followed by very long absences where I couldn't even face it. Procrastination and fierce self-criticism were not good for the productive process and things were soon out of date with places opening and closing and then with moving abroad to work it got even harder to keep up with what was happening.

The original idea was for a series of short essays about pubs and beer experiences inspired by the many photographs I had taken in pubs over the years. That then evolved into more of a conventional memoir with each chapter referring to particular beery places and moments in time. Looking back at the photos to jog the memory, it soon became apparent how much has changed. The mid-1990s don't seem that long ago, but they are a generation ago. Mobile phones were rare and there was no Internet. Some of the pub paraphernalia, brands and advertising in photos looked like antiquities. I was seeing more pubs that I used to know with 'To Let' or 'For Sale' signs on them for a while or were suddenly demolished. It really got me thinking just how much the beer world had changed.

The old business model for pubs and breweries that I first knew has long disappeared. One small group of dominant pub owners has been replaced with another small group of dominant owners with at times disastrous results. Huge and historic names in brewing have gone, as have many of the beers that they produced. On one extreme, huge global corporations produce bland, mass-market products and on the other, new generations of entrepreneurs full of creativity, vision and new ideas have brought a vast range of beers to the market and there is more choice than ever. There are hundreds of breweries making a vast range of beers and whilst there is no doubt that lots of pubs have closed, some terrific new places are opening and breathing new life into the pub.

Walking into a decent pub and ordering and drinking a pint of beer is as enjoyable now as it has always been. Decision-making can at times be more pressurised given the amount of choice on offer in so many places. Things were so much simpler in the late 1980s. As well as the choice, the damage to the wallet is also much more significant, especially in places that think exposed bricks and 1930s style lightbulbs or the use of the words 'craft' or 'artisan' can justify an extra pound or more on a pint. But, minor gripes apart, ordering that pint of beer, watching it settle with the creamy head slowly rising to the top before taking that first sip never fails to be one of life's simplest pleasures.

Few will have been as lucky to serve their beer apprenticeship in a pub as wonderful as the one I did. It served superb hand-pulled beer and was everything a pub should be. Thankfully, despite all the changes that have occurred over the years and the contrasting fortunes of other pubs, it is still going strong. It hasn't changed since I went in for the first time in 1988, apart from the lack of cigarette smoke, and this lack of change is one of the many reasons people love it. It remains as wonderful now as it was back then. It is almost identical in décor, ambience and, most importantly, it still serves terrific beer.

The beer we drank and this pub that we drank it in became an important part of our youth. It remains part of who we are and our shared heritage, not just a distant memory. We still miss it and when any of us return there after increasingly longer absences the second thing that is done after the pint is ordered is a picture is taken and sent to show what the others are missing. I can only visit a couple of times a year these days but it still gives me the same thrill walking through the door, heading to the bar, ordering a pint and taking the first mouthful of delicious beer. At one time, it would have been Tetley Bitter, the beer that turned us on to cask ale, but that has long gone. Whether the beer on offer is from Somerset or Shetland, it is always beautifully served in perfect condition and one is never enough.

So, there was an idea and a creative urge, but there was then the problem of producing it. It didn't take me long to realise that trying to write a book is really, really tough. Most of the time, it has been an enjoyable and almost therapeutic experience. Some great times have been recalled, though sadly plenty have had to be left out. They would have made good stories, but some things are best left in the memories of those involved.

The result is not a detailed history of beer, pubs and brewing over the years. That was never the intention. As may become apparent, I am not an expert. I am merely someone who likes beer and fancied writing a book. This is merely my take on the subject. It is a personal view on my time with beer. It isn't a serious appraisal of beer over the period and I don't get distracted or bogged down with the big issues over the last thirty years in the industry, such as pubcos, the Campaign for Real Ale (CAMRA), or, heaven forbid, the craft beer debate which *still* seems to get people very excited. It is intended as a light-hearted look at thirty years of going to the pub, drinking beer and getting pissed.

For those wanting something a bit more 'serious' about the world of beer, there are plenty of other good books out there. If you haven't discovered them already, I would highly recommend Boak and Bailey's *Brew Britannia* (2014) which is an excellent take on the last forty or so years of British brewing.

For a much broader view of beery history and arguably the book that set the trend for modern beer writing, there is the also excellent *Man Walks into a Pub* by Pete Brown (2006) which condenses the long history of beer into a book that is very accessible and at times very funny. Although I don't buy his books any more, credit where credit is due there is no doubt that his first book is a classic.

I have never met him, but this social media age allows us to fall out with people we have never met. Brown had an interesting blog in the late 2000s which I still read and on many things beer-related he does talk an awful lot of sense. It was on that modern battleground that is Twitter that I fell out with him. I can take or leave Twitter. I get why people use it to find out about things or people you might be interested in. I understand its use as a marketing tool. What I don't understand is just how much importance people place on it and how excited people can get about things people tweet about. If you are interested in beer then joining Brown's seventeen thousand followers is a good way to discover what he is up to, read interesting articles he might share or find out about events that you might be interested in going to.

But thanks to Twitter, I fell out with Brown 'virtually.' He may well be a perfectly nice bloke, he's certainly a good writer and he is very knowledgeable about all things beer. However, his tweeting increasingly strayed into topics away from beer and, on occasion, to controversial and divisive ones. Whatever his views are, he is more than entitled to them, but when you instantly share them to thousands of people in a hundred and forty characters or less, not everyone might agree with you and there is a chance you might rub people up the wrong way, which is what happened. After buying the first four of his books I haven't bought one since. I am sure that he will cope without my occasional £8.99.

Social media gives everyone else the opportunity to spout their two penn'orth, often people far less articulate than Brown but equally opinionated. It is a nasty, aggressive platform much of the time with everyone having their own opinion yet being incredibly intolerant of other people's views. Everyone is offended by everyone else these days and it can be both fascinating and depressing scrolling through some threads as people 'communicate' with people that they don't know and have never met in ways that would result in a punch in the face in the real world.

It was surprising, to me at least, that the subject of beer was no different to immigration, terrorism, Katie Hopkins or the other controversial topics that get people wound up and angrily bashing their keyboards. It isn't difficult to find angry threads about beer on social media and I came out of several Facebook groups because I was tired of the same old arguments and vitriol. It is astonishing just how much time and negative energy people put into arguing that day is night about a beer or pub rather than accepting that individual 'A' likes beer 'B' in pub 'C' and you don't.

I have tried to steer clear of controversy in this tale, but there one or two opinions in here. If you don't share my views on Wetherspoon's or Tetley for example, then so be it, I'll live with it. There is one opinion that runs through much of the book where my opinion will not change, and that is that the Tetley Bitter of the late 1980s and early 1990s served in the pubs of West Yorkshire was the best beer ever. Fact! However good many of the new beers are, and I have my favourites, nothing will ever replace that wonderful beer.

It was a consistently wonderful pint around our early haunts. After some false starts with dodgy lager, it was Tetley Bitter and the Tetley pubs of

Halifax that provided our early beer education and set the 'bar' for us against which all other beers were compared. It was such a great beer and served perfectly in the pubs that we were discovering. Admittedly, there wasn't much other choice for beer at the time, but even so it was far better than the competition. It has never been replicated and we will never see it again.

The Tetley name might still exist but the product that we knew has long gone, along with all the other early beers. On the rare occasion that I see Tetley cask ale on the bar, I repeatedly fall into the same trap. Every time I see it, I order it thinking that *this time* it will taste even remotely like the Tetley that we used to drink. Even when the beer has been well kept and well served and the pub's other beers are good, therefore excluding bad cellar keeping, it never, ever comes close to how it was. The taste is not there, it is always bland, tasteless and I am always disappointed.

It was in decline in cask form long before the move away from its Leeds home. It was getting harder to find and the last decent pint I had was in one of the last long-standing Tetley pubs we knew way back in 2000. It was losing its influence, certainly in my part of West Yorkshire anyway, with changes in pub ownership and the rise in the popularity of beers produced by the new start-up independent breweries. The great Tetley taste hasn't been replicated in Burton or wherever it is now brewed. Tetley was a Leeds beer, a Yorkshire beer, but like so many other beers of the time, it remains in name only now that it is brewed miles from the original brewery.

It is easy to look back approaching middle age and lament the lost beers and lost pubs of the past. Whilst you could get four pints for a fiver and still have change for some chips on the way home, there can be no doubt that the choice of beers available and the love and thought that goes into their production in the many small breweries has never been better. The market is full of great (and some not so great) beers from brewers of varying size. Some of the more established operators are now developing their own pub estates, just like small local breweries did over a hundred years ago as things go full circle back to small, local producers, with some brewing in the back room or the cellar of the pub, much like the beer-houses of old. Every week, someone seems to be opening a small brewery from their garage or cellar, dreaming of getting their beers out in to an increasingly crowded marketplace.

Long gone are the days when there might only be a choice of a couple of different beers in a whole town. Choice is good, but I do miss the traditional tied-house brewery owned pubs that I first ventured into. Walking into a tied pub, you knew exactly what to expect on the bar. The pubs were managed by often long-term managers and they were supported by the breweries that owned them. Now, so many pubs are milked dry by a faceless property or investment company, only interested in getting every bit of cash out of them with revolving doors of tenants that struggle to deliver on ever increasing demands.

Even as thousands of traditional pubs have closed over the years, new ones are opening, often offering a different interpretation of the pub and the beer we drink in them. Things change constantly and at times quickly and hopefully young people starting out on their beery journey now will be discovering their very own Tetley Bitter and their own special pub. Maybe in another twenty-five years they will be the ones reflecting on how such-and-such an IPA doesn't taste the same anymore or that isn't it great that the exposed brick, wooden floored, craft beer bar that they first went into is still going strong and hasn't changed over the years.

A lot has changed over the last thirty years. A lot will change over the next thirty, and probably at a much faster rate. Whether *Viz* are still selling their t-shirts are not, I have no doubt that beer will still be great. It will probably be different again, but I'm sure that it will still be great. But for now, it is 1987, Thatcher is in her pomp, there's a Cold War on, and I'm approaching my sixteenth birthday.

2 STARTING OUT

My relationship with beer began with that irresponsible and corrupting youth organization called the Boy Scouts. As well as the traditional activities like knot tying, map-reading and camping in decrepit leaking tents that looked old enough to have been with Baden-Powell on Brownsea Island, it was also in the Scouts that I first went to the pub and drank my first beer.

I had been involved with the local group from the moment I was old enough to join the Cub Scouts, moving onto the Boy Scouts when I was eleven. I didn't miss many Thursday night patrol meetings which were held at the nearby church hall. It was through the Scouts that I developed my lifelong love of the great outdoors and the peace and solitude of the hills and moors of northern England thanks to the regular trips to the Yorkshire Dales, Peak District and Lake District. All three places remain among my favourite places in the world, provided that the rain holds off. Whilst the love of the hills remains, many of the skills that I learned have long since slipped from memory. Whilst it can still occasionally be useful to know how to tie a reef knot or a clove hitch, thankfully I've not had the subsequent need to cook an egg in a hollowed-out orange on a camp fire. They really did taste as revolting as they sound.

As I approached sixteen, my time in the Boy Scouts was coming to an end and it was time to decide whether to leave altogether or to move on to the next age group who were then known as Venture Scouts. There were a few of us at the leaving stage and we decided to move up collectively to the next level, a bit of safety in numbers, and I was nervously looking forward it.

I have no idea how they operate these days or even how popular the Scouts are with the youth of today, even with Bear Grylls as Chief Scout. I wonder if they still parade at the beginning of each meeting and unfurl and salute the union flag whilst reciting 'I promise that I will do my best, to do my duty to God and the Queen....' and so on. I gather that the traditional

Easter holiday 'Bob-a-Job Week' that we used to do has long gone, but they still do some healthy outdoor activities because I have seen groups in kayaks on local rivers before now, though I noticed that they wear life-jackets these days.

As a senior Scout, and patrol leader, aged sixteen I was in a group that still included new entrants at eleven years old who seemed so young. Moving up was going to be the opposite. We were going to be the kids in the group and the rest of the group were the ones who seemed enormously grown up. What I didn't quite realise at the time was just how grown up they were. They were a long-standing group of friends who had been connected with the Scouts and the Girl Guides for years (Venture Scouts were a mixed group). Instead of leaving at eighteen, they were still involved with the group and one or two of them were as 'old' as twenty. They helped with the junior groups and still came to their Thursday night meetings as a social thing as much as anything else because after their relatively short meeting they would head to the nearby pub. As part of the transition to the senior group, those of us about to join were invited along to one of their regular weekends away in the Yorkshire Dales.

The destination was a regular venue for these weekends away. It was the gorgeous village of Conistone which was set in a particularly peaceful stretch of Wharfedale in the Yorkshire Dales, just off the road between Grassington and Kettlewell. I've not been there for over ten years, but on the last visit it remained very much as it was back in 1987, a beautiful, unspoiled village of rugged stone cottages and farmhouses. Back then there was a church, a tiny combined post office and village store and vintage road signs still proclaiming its location in the West Riding of Yorkshire. The local government changes of 1974 swept away the historic Ridings, subsequently placing the village in North Yorkshire. It was a working agricultural village and wasn't really on the tourist trail beyond providing access to Grassington Moor through a limestone ravine behind the church. There was no pub and it seemed as if the whole village was in bed by 9pm it was so quiet.

It was and remains a classic Yorkshire Dales rural idyll so I'm sure the hard-working Dales village folk were thrilled when it was announced in the early 1980s that the other church in the village, a redundant Methodist chapel, was to be converted into what they now call a 'youth resource centre' by the West Yorkshire Methodist District. The church had closed in 1980 and was a typical Victorian Methodist chapel building, functional and unspectacular and a little out of place among the much older stone farmhouses.

I have very fond memories of the place and had been there on numerous occasions in the mid-1980s before this trip. It seemed fine at the time as a cheap and cheerful bunkhouse, rather than a youth resource centre, but looking back at some photos it is surprising just how basic it was. In what would have been the vestry at the back of the church there was a very small dining area supplied from a tiny galley kitchen completely unsuited to group catering. There was no lounge area, no radio and no TV.

What would have been the main hall of the church was divided rather crudely by a breeze block wall around eight feet high into male and female sleeping areas. There was no ceiling on the sleeping areas and it got cold at night throughout the year but especially so in Winter because what little heating there was became lost in the open expanse of the church hall. The centre is still going and, looking at its website, it remains basic but it has at least upgraded and moved into the realms of moderately more comfortable group accommodation with some improvements to the decor and furniture. Although I had visited the chapel as early as 1984, by the time of this 1987 trip, the downstairs bedrooms did have ceilings which allowed for some heat to be retained as well as creating space for more sleeping accommodation upstairs which put even more pressure on the limited catering facilities.

Nowadays, it might be the kind of building and location that features in one of those TV programmes where clueless affluent city dwellers pay a huge amount of cash to create some amazing home with every move and disaster filmed and so the Methodist church surely deserves some credit for not cashing in their asset over the subsequent years. Its original mission has been retained and no doubt thousands of young people have passed through the building over the last almost forty years. If even a fraction of them have gained the love for the Dales and the great outdoors that I have, then it has surely served its purpose.

It was popular for these trips because it was cheap and just over an hour's drive from Halifax. Because the Venture Scouts were linked to a Methodist church, they enjoyed priority access to the building and there were several trips a year. The main activity on these trips was usually a day long hike on the Saturday over the rugged limestone moorland around Grassington. This trip was no exception and after a bracing February day tramping around the moors, it was back to the chapel for a lukewarm shower followed by a one-pot hot meal which was just about all the kitchen could handle.

Once everyone was cleaned and fed there was the dilemma about what to do for the rest of the evening. It was February, it was dark early and there wasn't much to do at the hostel apart from sit around and drink tea with the only in-house entertainment being numerous battered board games with missing pieces. It was a Saturday night and most the group were comfortably beyond eighteen years old with a pub within walking distance. They knew what they wanted to do and it seemed natural for them to go down the road for an hour or so which is what they frequently did before us kids turned up on their trip. Thankfully the leader of the group was willing to trust us with his reputation and he agreed to take the whole group, including those of us that were significantly under-age, down the road to the Tenants' Arms which was a ten-minute walk away under the shadow of the impressive Kilnsey Crag at the side of the Kettlewell road.

Maybe Scout groups go to the pub these days on their weekends away, but I have my doubts. I'm sure stories of Scout leaders and fifteen-year-old boys drinking alcohol on trips to the countryside wouldn't go down too well if the *Daily Mail* heard about it. Plus, even the tough *'Think 21'* campaigns often in place in pubs to deter under-age drinkers are being replaced by even more Puritan *'Think 25'* schemes. Things weren't quite as strict back then, or at least they didn't seem to be. Pubs seemingly operated their own policy on serving based on their own judgement, especially those out in the countryside like the Tenants' Arms, far from the prying eyes of the local constabulary.

And so, in February 1987 at the tender age of fifteen, a few days before my sixteenth birthday, I wandered into a pub on a Scout trip and nervously ordered my first beer, not even really knowing what to order. To my amazement, the barman served me without question and shortly afterwards my pint appeared on the bar. I handed over my money, got my change from a £1 coin, moved away from the bar and sat down with the others. I sipped it slowly, making it last as well as getting used to the taste. When it was finished and I was feeling confident enough to try again, I went back to the bar. Again, I was served without an issue and I had no idea how. He must have surely that known I was under-aged. I didn't think I looked eighteen as a badly dressed, gangly fifteen-year-old, but I was tall and I didn't have bum fluff on my face which possibly helped. I didn't want to push my luck though and I quit whilst I was ahead without ordering a third.

***

That night in Kilnsey wasn't my first time in the pub though. Indeed, one of my earliest childhood memories was sitting outside a pub. My actual earliest memory was pushing my sister out of her pushchair (I think accidentally) in the car park at the Halifax Asda, or 'Queens' as it was called at the time. That was before it burnt down when the neighbouring empty mill caught fire like a lot of empty mills mysteriously seemed to do in the 1970s. More than the fall from the pram, the overriding memory is of someone rubbing a lump of butter on to the massive lump on her head. There was only moderate drama, no A&E, just a lump of butter.

But back to that early visit to the pub, I didn't go inside on that occasion. It was the scorching hot summer of 1976 and we had been out for a family walk. We waited outside whilst Dad went in to get the drinks. It wasn't something that happened very often and the moment was captured in some pictures of us sat outside the pub with our fizzy pop and crisps in the sunshine. The pub is still there, still open and relatively unchanged although the grass banking on which we were sat is now home to the modern phenomenon that is executive apartments.

The pub was the Standard of Freedom on Skircoat Green, just up the road from where we lived. It is now a well to do suburb made up of a mix of Victorian terraces, inter-war semis, huge semi-detached and detached houses and even a few small mansions. Before the Industrial Revolution the original community around the green was a very small rural outpost isolated from the larger settlement of Halifax a couple of miles north. The original green was set on a slight hill with a small cluster of densely packed cottages and cobbled courtyards which have survived creating an old-world charm to the area leading up to the green itself.

The pub was positioned at the top of a very steep thirst inducing climb up from Copley on the floor of the Calder Valley. It was here, where we were chomping our crisps outside what was then known as the Waggoner's Inn, that in 1840 a group of Chartists gathered on their way to a meeting. Halifax and neighbouring towns were industrialising rapidly and the Chartists were early agitators for political and electoral reform. They must have found a receptive ear because the story goes that the landlord made a favourable speech, declaring 'The People of Skircoat Green shall join in that march of freedom and I will raise the Standard of Freedom at this inn.' The name was adopted and a hundred and seventy-five years later the pub is still open and it still retains the name. Local history documented in pub names is just one of the things that makes them great.

That was about as close as it got to the pub as a child. My parents weren't really interested and were busy making ends meet and with a couple of young kids to bring up. Mum was never that bothered anyway as she found them far too smoky. Dad, allegedly, had his moments as a young man and especially as a student in York in the late 1960s, stories which didn't emerge until many years later. Dad's contact with the pub from the 1970s until his illness prevented it forty years later was going for a late drink with a friend once a week (and collecting forty years of beer mats in the process). This was quite a contrast to the man who not that many years previously as a student had sat in the open rear doors of his mate's small van driving round the streets of York after a session skimming stolen ashtrays off the road. And some people think alcohol-related anti-social behaviour is a modern thing.

His father was a bit more of a frequent pub goer, especially in his retirement. I loved the trips down to my grandparents as a child. They had reluctantly relocated in their mid-fifties from a picturesque north Staffordshire village to the industrial grime of South Yorkshire. The brickyard he managed was being closed and he was offered a transfer to a site near Doncaster. As a sweetener, the company bought them a substantial red-brick detached house with an enormous L-shaped garden with trees, bushes, two sheds ('top shed' and the 'half-way house') and a garage at the bottom. It was a wonderful play area and even though things seem much bigger to a child, it really was big, especially given that we lived in a small terraced house with a tiny back yard. I was very adept at entertaining myself and I could lose myself for hours in the garden, building improvised tree-houses from all manner of flimsy materials and sheets of asbestos that were lying around. I could spend all day playing in the garden and hanging out with Grandad which usually involved something educational, anything from explaining about his plants and vegetables to finding rope and tying knots to looking for the moles which were blighting his lawns. At night, I would be allowed to stay up much later than normal watching programmes like *Not the Nine O'clock News* with Pamela Stephenson's *American Express* sketch making quite an impression on a nine-year-old (it's on YouTube).

At around half past nine he would get washed and changed, put on a shirt, tie and blazer and head off to the pub. He wasn't heading to a nearby local though. Instead he was driving a few miles to the nearby pit village of Edlington, home to one of the large collieries of the South Yorkshire coalfield, the Yorkshire Main. The pub was further down the road from the colliery on the outskirts of the village and was the White Greyhound, commonly referred to as 'The Greyhound.' Grandma never went with him. I'm not sure that she was ever asked but she had no interest in pubs or alcohol. Her upbringing had been one where pubs were no place for a decent woman and drunkenness was frowned upon. At Christmas, she would occasionally relax that rule and have a bottled snowball, but not every Christmas because that could be habit-forming.

After goodness knows how many pints, he would then get back into his car, a blue 'F' registered Ford Cortina Mk 2 and drive home. I can still see it parked on the narrow drive next to the kitchen. It seemed an enormous car at the time, an almost American like saloon compared to Dad's Austin 1100. I don't know how many pints he had but he always got back and got the car in the drive unscathed. If we were still up, which was not uncommon because Grandma wasn't strict about bedtimes, he'd then come in and sit down and open his home brew. He would let me have a small glass of it which I never enjoyed but always accepted because it seemed so naughty. The home brewed beer was certainly better than the home brewed wine that sat bubbling on the hearth all year round and that I was also occasionally allowed to try. It was hardly surprising it tasted so grim given my undeveloped taste buds and that it was made from whatever nettles and berries he could find in his garden.

If I was there at the weekend there might be a Saturday evening treat and Grandma and I would be taken to the Greyhound for a drink. Well,

Grandad went to the Greyhound for a drink because I was to experience what was a common 1970s pub experience for a child; sitting in the back of a car in a pub car park with pop and crisps. Grandma and I would sit on the back seat of the Cortina whilst Grandad went inside to get the supplies before he disappeared back in to the pub for his pint. I vividly remember people talking to us, other women who stayed with us in the car park rather than going inside, probably the wives of the other regulars Grandad knew who came out with the husbands once a week on Saturday night, only to spend it in the car park talking to us. I'm not sure if children were allowed in the pub, whether it was that Grandma didn't want me being in a pub or whether it was that she didn't want to be in herself. After finishing his pints he'd then drive us home on what were dark back roads - with no seat belts, obviously.

Inadvertently passing through the area in 2003 for the first time in years I rounded the corner and was faced with the Greyhound for the first time since the late 1970s. It was a tragic site. The car park was abandoned and there were weeds and small trees growing out of the building. It had been closed for some time and it had been twenty years since Grandad had died and the Greyhound had dropped off the radar. No-one else in the family had any interest in going there. It was a road I never normally needed to use and so it caught me off guard. It was such a shock to see something that had figured so much in family nostalgia as a sad ruin. The colliery had long gone, the village was experiencing tough times and now the village's largest pub had gone.

Fast forward another few years and times had changed again. It had been a big pub with a huge car park which made it desirable again, but not for use as a pub. The inevitable happened and the pub was bought, flattened and executive homes now occupy the site. There is no trace that the Greyhound ever existed.

All this was a far cry from the late 1950s when the pub was built. It was no doubt a huge statement of intent and optimism from the nearby Barnsley Brewing Company. They brewed at the Oakwell Brewery in the town and they had a sizeable pub estate in the 1950s. It was a large purpose-built roadside pub on the edge of the village on a spacious site with a large car park to benefit from the boom in car ownership (and more relaxed attitudes towards drink driving).

As well as the emerging market of car owners, there were also no doubt plenty of men with cash in their pockets and a thirst to quench. In the 1950s Edlington was a still a colliery village dominated by the Yorkshire Main colliery where output at one time was a million tonnes of coal a year. It was still a pit village when Grandad died and it wasn't until the following year that the proposed closure of uneconomic pits triggered the miners' strike with staunch support around the South Yorkshire coalfield. The strike ended in 1985 and the colliery closed soon after. Apart from the huge winding wheel monument at the entrance to the light industrial estate that now occupies the site and some abandoned railway lines, no trace of the colliery remains.

The Greyhound saw change in the 1960s as the brewing industry began to see increased consolidations and takeovers. One of the breweries ambitiously expanding and creating a huge pub estate was the John Smiths brewery of Tadcaster, near York. The Barnsley Brewery was a 'small' regional brewer with two hundred and fifty pubs which is a big pub estate by many standards. Smiths acquired the Barnsley Brewery in 1961 and, despite promises to keep the brewery open, they ran it down before finally closing it in 1976. Barnsley's brewing heritage was re-established with the short-lived Barnsley Brewing Company in the 1990s. When that brewery soon folded, an employee went on to form the Acorn Brewery, also in the town, re-creating recipes from the original Barnsley Brewery and it has gone from strength to award-winning strength.

The first pub I remember going into has also long gone. On the regular journeys to South Yorkshire from Halifax we would head towards the M62 going past the Salterhebble canal basin where, somewhat isolated in what had since become a busy junction, was the Calder and Hebble. The pub was named after the canal, or navigation as it technically was (a navigation being a combination of man-made stretches of canal and sections of navigable river) that ran underneath the road and past the pub. Life and limb had to be risked just getting into the place across two lanes of traffic accelerating onto the dual carriageway that started right outside the pub. The pub has long been demolished but it did provide a lasting memory because on the gable end facing traffic heading out of town was a large 'Double Diamond' sign. I have no idea why it stuck so clearly in the memory. I can only assume that maybe Double Diamond sounded exotic, or that it made me curious what a *Double* Diamond was. Although it was generally out of favour by the time I was going to the pub, people have assured me that Double Diamond was anything but exotic.

I don't know what the reason was for going in one day with the family because pub outings then were very rare. I just remember it being loud and intimidating and, sitting at a table and having no other view apart from the backs of men standing and talking loudly to each other, I didn't like it at all. How things would soon change.

By the mid-1980s, there were signs of progress, change and innovation in pubs, even in Halifax. More and more pubs were diversifying and offering food. At the regular family gatherings with the now-widowed Grandma, instead of picnics or eating at home as we had done in the past, we started going out more for a bar meal. The previously pub-avoiding Grandma came to love being taken for a run out in the car that ended up at a pub for a bar meal. To her, going out for a late lunch of a basket of scampi and chips was the height of sophistication and going to a pub to eat was very different from going to a pub to drink. These food-friendly pubs met with her approval with less smoke, less drunkenness and less bad language. The Colliers at nearby Elland was run by the Samuel Smiths brewery and in the mid-1980s it was an early favourite destination for these bar meals. They even built a conservatory on the side for this new wave of dining customers to take in the picturesque canal that ran next to the pub, provided you didn't glance over to the nearby power station and cooling towers a couple of miles away. It was a proper canal side pub where narrowboats would moor up right outside and there was a colourful collection of boats adding to the scene whilst the owners had a couple of pints. Sadly, the pub was badly affected by the Calder Valley floods on Boxing Day 2015 when the adjacent canal and nearby river both burst their banks. It was also affected by the previous 'once in a generation' storm and flood in 2013 which flooded the area. At the time of writing it is still closed and unlikely to re-open.

So, by the time I was in the Tenants' Arms in February 1987 and about to enjoy my first beer I had become a *little* bit more familiar with pubs, but I still knew absolutely nothing about beer.

3 EARLY DAYS

Although it seemed a hugely significant event at the time, memories of that first and second beer in the pub at Kilnsey quickly receded into memory. It would be several months before I ventured back into another pub and rather than being a customer, my next visit was to be working in one.

In the Summer of 1987 after finishing my 'O' levels I had time on my hands and I wanted to earn some money. I hadn't needed money for beer at this point, but I had discovered records and I needed to finance this new hobby. I already had a lucrative Sunday morning newspaper round, lucrative because it paid double time, but with the rest of the week to occupy over the holidays I ended up at one of the area's pub success stories of the 1980s, perched high on the hills above the nearby Sowerby Bridge.

The Hobbit had formally adopted its long-held nickname after an extensive refurbishment. Before this it was officially the West Bottom Tavern which was a pub that had developed from a nineteenth century beer-house. It got the name The Hobbit not from some spurious Tolkien connection but because of its location on Hob Lane and in the mid to late 1980s it was quite the place to go to. It was spacious, did good food and there was a dance floor, function room, a small hotel, a large car park and, importantly, a late licence. The pub has a terrific outlook, especially on a Summer evening with the less picturesque Sowerby Bridge in the valley bottom giving way to spectacular views of the rugged Pennine moors stretching away over to Lancashire. Apart from sitting outside and taking in the view which the Yorkshire weather didn't permit too often, I never quite understood the pub's popularity especially given the clutch burning difficulty involved in getting there up the steep and narrow lanes from Sowerby Bridge. Popular it was though and, hearing that they were looking for waiting staff, I gave them a call.

I was invited up for a chat and so I put on my smartest black trousers, a pair of Spencers which were a locally produced male teenage fashion staple around school at the time. They are still making handmade trousers in their Sowerby Bridge factory, but not for the schoolboy crowd any more. I caught the bus to Norland and from there I walked the mile or so down the hill to the pub. Without much of a chat a job was offered with instructions to turn up on the following Saturday night. I hadn't had many job interviews to compare it to, but it did seem remarkably easy. Suspiciously easy in fact.

It was to be an illuminating early introduction to working life beyond the simplicity of delivering newspapers. Saturday came and I headed back up to Norland on the bus resplendent in the Spencers and a white shirt with black slip on shoes, complete with tassels as was popular at the time, and probably with white socks. I walked down the hill from the bus in the rain all set to enter the world of the waiter. I was there in plenty of time and ready to be briefed because I didn't know the first thing about being a waiter, restaurants or food. Instead of a briefing, I was promptly sent into the kitchen, given an apron, shown the sink and told to get on with it.

It transpired that they had no real intention of hiring me as a waiter and the kitchen staff couldn't believe how gullible I had been. This kind of trick wasn't new apparently, especially over the holidays, and the turnover of dishwashing staff was apparently very high. I've never been averse to a bit of hard graft and getting my hands dirty, but kitchen work, especially doing the washing up, is grim. I suspected as much before I even walked in there and these suspicions were soon confirmed. It was hot, tiring, backbreaking work. I had no gloves, no mechanised dish-washer, no help and no break. Every single plate, bowl and piece of cutlery was washed by hand and, like every Saturday night up there at the time, it was really busy. When I ventured out of the kitchen to ask for a glass of water at the bar, the owner saw me and told me to get back in the kitchen and to ask one of the harassed waitresses to get one for me. It was a long, long, horrible night. I knuckled down and got through it, collected my wages and never went back.

Years later the Hobbit came up in conversation, in a pub of course, and the person I was talking to shared his Hobbit experience from a couple of years before mine. This young lad, who would also have been around fifteen or sixteen at the time, was also looking for some extra pocket money. With the Hobbit's bonfire night extravaganza approaching, they were looking for someone to steward the car park and direct cars in and out to try and ensure that Hob Lane didn't become too congested. Bonfire night at the Hobbit always attracted a good crowd.

Sitting on a hill facing north-west over to the Pennines and exposed to the cold winds that could blow off them, early November can be a bit 'parky' as they say. In other words, it was freezing cold. I can only hope that he went

22

prepared because once he started his shift he wasn't allowed back inside to thaw out, get a hot drink or even go to the toilet for the whole event which will have gone on for several hours. Not being one to complain, he just got on with it and did a seemingly competent job. Once the event was over and the car park was almost empty, he went to see the boss to check whether he was still needed and to collect his wages. The arrangement was for cash in hand as a one-off and he was looking forward to a nice reward for half freezing to death all night. A rate hadn't been agreed in advance and he just assumed he was going to be reasonably rewarded for his efforts. He was astonished when he was given his money. It was £1.50. This was about 1984 or 1985, but even then students could expect a little more than about forty pence an hour. I really wish he'd told him to stick it or even better, punched him in the face, but he didn't. He was so shocked, dumbfounded, and close to hypothermia that he just took it and left. He did relish in telling the story for years afterwards and besmirching their reputation to anyone that would listen. Needless to say, he also never went back.

My career as a waiter was put on hold and it never resumed. Instead I got to go and chat with nurses. As luck would have it, the newsagent that I did my Sunday paper round for asked me to cover the round his shop had at the local hospital. The elderly chap that normally did it was on holiday and so twice a day for two weeks I pushed a large, heavy, metal trolley full of newspapers, magazines, sweets and cigarettes around the wards. It was a lucrative round. Newspapers were still hugely popular with people buying two or three a day with all the morning papers and a couple of evening ones. A lot of people in some of the wards never struck me as being *that* poorly given that the amount of papers and magazines that they bought. Cigarettes were by far the best-selling item and I could sell cigarettes to patients at their bedside on a lung or a maternity ward. This really was eye opening because thankfully my contact with hospitals was negligible beyond occasionally visiting people in them.

I had been to A&E twice; the first time was to have a boil lanced that had developed on my wrist when I was eleven. Goodness knows how I ended up with a boil on my wrist, an ailment from a Dickens novel. Maybe it was the gruel and monthly baths that I endured at home, but somehow this enormous boil appeared on my right wrist, typically just before we were about to go on holiday. On a visit to my grandma she attempted an equivalently Dickensian treatment of a hot poultice to 'draw it out.' Whatever a poultice was, it wasn't pleasant and it didn't succeed in 'drawing it out.' Instead, it was off to the infirmary to see a man with a scalpel and have it lanced. I screamed the place down.

The second time was after coming off my push bike when I was thirteen at the appropriately named Cunning Corner, a fast-downhill double bend near Rishworth about eight miles out of town whilst out on a Sunday cycle with a local club. It was 1984 and so of course no-one was wearing a helmet. I clipped the kerb at speed and hit the ground head first resulting in an enormous egg on my head. Once a phone box had been found an ambulance was called. There was also a call home with the not very tactful opening line, before any greetings or explanation, of 'there's been an accident.' My parents later said that they nearly died on the spot. It was nothing too serious and after a couple of hours' observation and a tetanus jab in my backside I was on my way home.

Seeing hospital from the other side was illuminating. I went around all the wards and the psychiatric unit. It was a Victorian hospital that has since been rebuilt with the original circular wards now listed buildings and used for other purposes. At the end of these wards were lounges which had a TV and some high-backed chairs. It wasn't dissimilar to a student common room, just with more nightwear and drip stands. Patients on these wards bought cigarettes by the carton and they could smoke them in these lounges, not in a separate smoking lounge, but in the same lounge everyone else was using. It seems inconceivable now when you can't even smoke in a hospital car park, or even a pub, but patients could merrily smoke as much as they wanted then. It was good for business; the Silk Cut, but more so the B&H Superkings (bigger and better value for money) and Lambert & Butler (cheapest) used to fly out of the trolley.

It brought in about £60 a week for two weeks which in 1987 was more money than I had ever had. Even after buying a few records there was plenty of money left over. Things were beginning to change socially and I had made a new friend at school who was more urbane, self-assured and adventurous than me. He suggested going to the pub and so we started exploring the world of pubs and beer together. We didn't get even moderately drunk. We were going more out of curiosity and to see what pubs were like, a learning experience for both of us. We went to chat and feel both grown up and rebellious because we were still significantly under-age. We were both comfortably over six feet tall which may have helped us get served. Early destinations were chosen through a mixture of recommendation and curiosity. Thankfully, we lived in a nice part of town and so the chances of imminent death by walking into the wrong pub – which is what would happen if you believed some of the tales going around school at the time – was reduced, or so we hoped. It was in these neighbourhood pubs that we forged a lifelong friendship over these early, illicit beers.

Some of our earliest adventures that summer also involved camping in local woods where, after a trip to the off-licence - the 'offy' - you could drink beer and talk nonsense without any of the worries of going into the pub. Of course, you still needed to be eighteen to get beer from the offy but, like pubs, if you knew where to go then getting hold of beer was quite easy.

With it being the 1980s, there were some spectacularly drab mass-produced brands to choose from. We didn't know our way around the marketplace at the time and we were guided very much by a combination of price and some of the brilliant cinema and TV advertising at the time, but mainly by price. Our first forays into offy beer couldn't have been any more dreadful, or 1980s, because we chose the yellow canned Hofmeister with its cringe-worthy adverts fronted by George 'follow the bear', a character that could only have come out of the mid-1980s. We were young and we didn't know any different.

As well as following the bear into various woodland camp-sites, we also ventured into the pub and another late 1980s experience. This early exploring was in an area just up the road from where we lived called King Cross. It was blessed with numerous pubs along what was then a busy community shopping street a couple of hundred metres long on what had been the main artery out of town to the west until a by-pass had opened a few years earlier. At the time, there were six pubs and even now four of them remain open. A short walk from the main drag of King Cross was the Allan Fold. This was a large art-Deco style pub in a prominent position built in the 1930s for the local Websters brewery. Its elevated position on the valley side allowed for large windows giving fabulous views over the valley and across to the hilltop village of Norland. When it was built the view perhaps wasn't quite so clear with smoke being belched from the mill chimneys of Sowerby Bridge in the valley bottom but the Clean Air Act and industrial decline had since corrected that. On a sunny day, the outlook was splendid.

It was also another hugely popular place at the time. Much like the Hobbit, it was one of the 'go-to' places of the period. There was a large open area inside to allow for the vertical drinking in front of the bar as well as a pool room and a small dance floor. There was also a late licence. There would appear to be an emerging trend between late licences and popular venues of the time.

We certainly weren't in the late-night disco dancing crowd, but we did occasionally sneak in there during the afternoon in the school holidays before it got too busy. Without casting aspersions on the clientele of the time, there was a slight air of menace as the evening crowd began to arrive, although that could have been our nervous, under-aged, inexperienced paranoia. Nothing did happen of course. We kept ourselves to ourselves and stayed out of trouble. We didn't spill anyone else's pint or look at anyone else's bird. We would slip into what would have been the snug and find a seat. Convinced we were right there at the cutting edge of 1980s trends, we would then order American lager. We really did think that was the cool thing to do. In a town that we were yet to discover was full of amazing cask ale, we ordered draught American lager. It was Miller

Genuine Draft and was a brand that even we knew in our limited experience was difficult to find at the time in a town that was almost a duopoly of breweries, each supplying their own non-American lagers. The Allan Fold was the only place we knew that sold it and we really did think we were being trend-setters in our own little way. Every other pub in town seemed to be selling Australian lager and there we were, bucking the trend and drinking American.

This was at the tail end of the popularity of American football being shown on Channel 4 and maybe the marketers were playing to that audience. The mid-1980s had really seen the arrival of lager as a mainstream drink and the draft market, at least in Halifax, was dominated by Australian brands. Miller Genuine Draft was a relatively new drink anyway having only been introduced in 1985 and, besides the hard to find Budweiser, it was the only other American beer we were aware of. We thought we were cool though and that was all that mattered at the time.

We felt emboldened by our Miller time in the Allan Fold and our confidence in going to the pub and our enjoyment of it developed. We still weren't eighteen (we weren't even seventeen), but we were getting served everywhere we went and we started going out a bit more at the weekends once we returned to school to start the lower sixth form.

An early social scene began to develop and there was a growing group of other people who had found Saturday jobs and had some money in their pockets who were starting to venture out. People weren't interested in places like the Allan Fold, regardless of its late licence. People wanted to be young and trendy and that meant a whole new experience. It meant going 'into town.'

4 ON THE TOWN

Halifax town centre is a small unassuming almost grid-like collection of mainly Victorian streets which rises westwards up an escarpment from the Hebble Brook. It was by the brook that the original town developed around the historic minster which dates from the 1400s. The original settlement is now almost non-existent as the railways and industrialization cleared land, followed by council bulldozers after the war leaving very little trace except a 17th century pub next to the Minster.

Although a historic settlement, the town centre very much reflects the town's rapid growth in the Victorian era based on the textile trade. The town has managed to retain much of its stunning Victorian architecture despite the best intentions of the council's bulldozers in the 1960s, especially if you look up above the mobile phone, charity and vape shopfronts that are sadly prevalent.

There are some unique and completely under-utilised gems like the Piece Hall, built in 1779 as a pre-industrial era cloth market which is currently being 'regenerated' and is due to open in late 2017 already twelve months behind schedule. There is also one of the most elaborate cast iron and glass covered Victorian markets in the north of England (which could also do with some love and investment) and an impressive town hall designed by the architect of the Houses of Parliament with the words 'Fear God Always' carved into stone and glaring down on the town.

There were also a lot of pubs. Not only were there a lot of them, with the town centre being very small, they were also very close together. By the mid-1980s they were attracting large crowds and the town centre was an incredibly popular place for drinkers, especially at the weekend. The pubs were very diverse. There were pubs for people in suits, students, rugby players and rock music fans. There were loud pubs, quiet ones, smart ones and scruffy ones. There was something for everyone and the town centre only takes a couple of minutes to walk from end to end and top to bottom so it was easy to move around them. In that compact little space, you didn't have to walk far at all before you found another one. There were so many pubs that more than one pub bore at the time would trot out that there were more pubs per square foot in Halifax town centre than in any other town in West Yorkshire / Yorkshire / northern England / the whole country depending which pub bore was talking to you. I have never verified the claim, which was regularly heard, but over the years in subsequent conversations with pub bores all over the country, there are plenty of other places making the same claim to fame. Regardless of whether Halifax held the record or not, there was no shortage of somewhere to get a pint.

Amazingly, considering the sorry looking state of the town these days, the town and its pubs had such a reputation in the mid to late 1980s that it was a magnet for weekend drinkers from around Yorkshire and even from across the north of England. At weekends, it would not be unusual to see coaches from places like Blackburn, Burnley and even as far away as Newcastle coming to Halifax for a night on the town. With a lot of pubs, half a dozen nightclubs, a good supply of curry houses and a couple of kebab shops, this seemingly unfashionable town had a brief moment as a weekend destination for party people where you could stumble short distances from one pub to another followed by either a dance or a fight in one of several nightclubs before spilling kebab sauce down your shirt as you fell asleep on the coach home. There was no real concerted attempt to market the town and push its potential as a night-time destination, it just seemed to happen naturally and the vast majority of pubs had been there for years. At the peak of this trend, there would be hundreds of people wandering the streets especially at the top of the town around Fountain Street and Bull Green where there was a cluster of popular pubs. The under-resourced taxi rank on George Square in the centre of town became notorious for late night brawling and black marias were never far away.

As well as the long-established pubs, there were one or two new additions. One of these new additions wasn't really a pub as such, I guess it would be classed as a bar rather than a pub because it was in the lower level of an imposing building on Fountain Street. In fact, it was in the cellar of an old-world former gentlemen's club from an era when gentlemen's clubs didn't even allow women in, never mind let them take their clothes off.

Maggie McFly's was not, as the name might suggest, some dreadful Irish theme pub, but was part of an early revival to put a modern twist on the traditional pub. It was a cellar-style bar but it had old fashioned wooden booths and vintage advertising signs combined with exposed brick, wooden flooring and thoughtful lighting. It also served good hand-pulled beer and it was soon a popular destination for the office and smarter dressed crowd as well as sixth formers looking to start going out into town.

In those early weeks and months of the lower sixth towards the end of 1987 it soon became the established convention to meet in Maggie's at around 8.30pm. It was a general, open thing that anyone that was out could meet there. There were regular faces on those early outings and plenty of people that dipped in and out of this emerging scene, including myself and Bob. It depended on who was out and what the mood was as to how the evening progressed. In those early days, it was predictable and after a couple of pints in Maggie's we would move on to the Brass Cat. This was a short walk away and was another modern pub, but rather than being created from new like Maggie's, it was a complete re-build of a much older pub. The old Brass Cat had an unpleasant reputation until the Tetley brewery that owned it decided to gut it and double its size by putting a huge conservatory on the back and re-modelling the yard beyond it. It was light, airy and fashionable and it served good Tetley beer. It was always packed at the weekend. There wasn't much time for a pub crawl because after meeting at 8.30pm and maybe a stop at the Brass Cat, we would then aim to be in our destination before 10.30pm to avoid both the queue and the entry fee.

There was choice, of sorts, about where to go. We had missed the legendary Kibbutz, full of Goths and alternative types that had closed not long before we started venturing out. There was the Coliseum, an expensive, glitzy conversion of a former cinema run by a national leisure company, but it was avoided. It was all Lacoste shirts, slacks and lots of hair gel, although upstairs they had created what at the time was quite a unique bar for the town in Maine Street, a US themed 'street' bar with cobbles, pavements and trees. There was a deceptive mirror at the far end which successfully created an impression of making the place seem much bigger but which was also frequently walked into given the positioning of the gents' toilet door right next to it. They also served Miller Genuine Draft, but we'd moved on from that.

There was also Ritzy's, Denny's, the Cats' Bar and the Acapulco – all cheaper, nastier, shabbier versions of the Coliseum with questionable reputations and an even greater likelihood of casual violence. Denny's became a good place for sixth form parties due to their very casual approach to serving under-age drinkers but none of them had any redeeming features. Ritzy's soon disappeared and became a Yates' Wine Lodge (when Yates' Wine Lodges were still nice and had carpet and served a range of coffees, teas, wines and ports) whilst Denny's was housed in a vile 1960s brutalist block which was recently demolished to make way for a car park. The survivor is, surprisingly, the Acapulco which keeps going, allegedly one of the longest continually open nightclubs in the country. It was also recently voted number three in a poll of the nation's worst nightclubs. It looks tattier than ever above a long-closed Chinese restaurant with the street outside still frequently resembling a war zone on weekend evenings. We avoided all of them because in those early days of going out we had Crossleys' Bar.

It was in the most unusual of places. To get there meant walking the best part of half a mile out of the town centre and then turning down a cobbled road past a car showroom and under the large and minimally lit North Bridge. This led into the former industrial complex that was at one time the carpet mills of John Crossley and Sons, frequently cited as being the largest carpet factory in the world at its peak and proud suppliers of carpets to Concorde and the QE2 amongst many others. Crossleys' Carpets occupied a huge site that had grown from humble origins in a small building using the Hebble Brook as its first source of power at the beginning of the nineteenth century. Rapid growth in the Industrial Revolution caused the company to spread further up the valley floor as well as skyward due to the restricted space available creating huge, soot stained buildings with large chimneys belching out black smoke that typified the dark satanic mills of Victorian industry in the north of England.

By the 1980s size, tradition and past glories didn't matter and neither did the fact that you supplied the carpets for Concorde. It didn't make you immune from the changes affecting so much of British manufacturing. Like so many other traditional industries in the town the complex, by then owned by Carpets International, closed in 1983 after years of decline as foreign manufacturers made carpets cheaper elsewhere on modern machinery. Looking at pictures of some of the Halifax mills taken in the 1970s they did not look that dissimilar to pictures of mills taken in the 1870s, though with fewer fingerless children crawling into the fix machines on fourteen hour shifts.

The early descendants of the founding Crossleys had long taken their money to settle in their country pile in Suffolk with at least one of them becoming very much part of the Establishment as Baron Somerleyton. Other members of the Crossley family got into politics both locally and in Westminster as well as running the family business and later becoming philanthropists. Their donations are evident around the town with churches, schools, alms-houses and parks built from their benevolence and they also provided a lot of the financing for the town hall. They were also behind the breath-taking building that was the Crossley Orphanage, later to become the Crossley and Porter School and later still the Crossley Heath School that Bob and I attended.

Just as the colliery villages near my grandparents lost their identity with the closure of their pits a few years later, the town lost a big part of its identity with the closure of Crossleys' Carpets, seen as the final nail in the coffin for the town's traditional industries, many of whom were dependent on the textile trade. Halifax had been a world leader in the production of worsted cloth which was stronger, finer, smoother and harder than conventional woollens. Dozens of other mills had also closed as did machine tool manufacturers, hauliers and other connected businesses. Thankfully there was diversification in the town's economy with finance, confectionery and brewing still producing nationally recognised brands which did help soften the blow, saving the town from the kind of decline other textile towns around the north were to suffer. With a working population of between five and six thousand at its peak, Crossleys' Carpets really was a place that everyone in the town knew someone who worked there.

Parts of the complex had already been demolished before the final closure as the site contracted and new roads were built, but a significant part of the site remained. On closure, it was quickly acquired by a couple of ambitious businessmen with a vision for urban regeneration. They gradually brought the buildings back to life with a mix of small business space, offices and cultural uses. Besides work space the site now includes a hotel, restaurants, art galleries and a theatre and it is claimed that as many people work there now as they did when it was a working mill.

One of the early businesses to open was a nightclub with the highly original name of Crossleys' Bar. It really was a strange place to open a nightclub, but maybe fitting given that this was a new vision for an old building, something different. Given the predictable nature of the nightclubs in the town centre, Crossleys' Bar was a revelation to teenagers in their early days of being out on the town. It was a relatively small former industrial building housed over three floors. After getting past the bouncers, which always proved surprisingly easy, there were a few steps which led down to the noise of the ground floor. There was a small bar on the left, the original metal supporting columns were in place and the dance floor was the original stone flagged floor. It was busy, noisy and dark and it belted out those dance floor filling classics of the late 1980s - Whitney Houston, Wet Wet Wet, The Bangles and the like, real 1980s gold. Whilst girls with big hair and white stilettos danced around their handbags on the ground floor, Crossleys' Bar also had variety. The second floor had vintage chairs, sofas and bookcases creating an almost lounge like environment providing a welcome break from the music for people to relax and chat. Upstairs again was another nightclub floor, but this one was much darker, louder and edgier both in terms of clientele and the music played. There was no chart music up there. This was where the cool kids listened to the rapidly emerging electronic 'house' music, a trend that, like many, managed to completely pass me by.

The variety gave the place an eclectic mix as people moved between floors and congregated in the quieter middle floor and in the outdoor area overlooking the brook on warmer evenings. Alternative types in jeans and leather jackets would mix with townies in shirts and slacks whilst smoking and having a breather, not that you had to go outside to smoke in those days of course. Beer was a whopping £1.10 a pint which I remember vividly because it was the first time I had paid over £1 for a pint of beer in my still short drinking career. It was terrible and widely rumoured to have been watered down.

Crossleys' Bar was a unique place with its three very different floors and mixed clientele. There were usually people inside that you knew, and there were others from school that didn't do the Maggie's meet. It began as something new and exciting but it didn't take long for the novelty to wear off and for it to start to lose its edge and its appeal. It was almost the same format each week with the same music being played in the same rotation. People are fickle and quickly move on to the next thing and it didn't take long for the numbers to drop off each time we went, not that we went every week.

My views towards it weren't helped by a couple of assaults. I have been punched in the face four times and two of those involved Crossleys' Bar. The first was completely unprovoked by someone in a group of people walking towards us whilst myself and a friend were walking back into town to go home. Given the long walk from town it did make you feel exposed if you weren't in a group and it put me off going there unless you knew you could leave with others. I used to walk all the way home and think nothing of it, but it was always the crossing of the town centre where trouble was more likely to occur. There was just the two of us and they shoved him and punched me. It was only one punch but it was enough to knock my glasses off and break the glass lens.

On another occasion, not long after, but by which time I was wearing contact lenses, I was much more dangerously sucker punched on the dance floor and fell and hit my head. The next thing I knew I woke up on my friend's couch the following morning and had got there walking and talking under my own steam. Thankfully my parents and his parents were on holiday. I had clearly been concussed because I had no recollection whatsoever of what happened beyond the dance-floor and after only a couple of pints I couldn't blame the amnesia on the beer. It wasn't even a hazy recollection; it was a complete blank.

Those incidents were already putting me off but it didn't take long before it really started to get quieter and quieter on Saturday nights. The beer started to taste even more watery and the cool kids on the top floor moved onto somewhere cooler. Then, one Saturday night in the Summer of 1988 we walked down to find the lights out and the door locked. We thought we had made a mistake with the timing but there were no signs of life and no cars in the car park. We shrugged our shoulders, turned around and went back into town. Crossleys' Bar never opened again.

There were rumours going around of course about drugs, money, the usual, though none seemingly with any substance and we were hardly in the loop as seventeen-year-old school kids. We briefly mourned its passing and did what you do when somewhere closes; you find somewhere else to go. In a way, the closing of Crossleys' Bar signified the end of our first era of going out and drinking beer. It signified the end of the 8.30pm meet in Maggie's because people were beginning to form their own groups and starting to do their own thing. By the time we started upper sixth a few weeks later more and more people were going out, but to different places and with different people. Bob and I were also about to split from the norm and make our own discovery, and it wasn't to be in the town centre.

5 THE WORLD'S BEST BEER AND PUB

Savile Park is an elegant and moderately affluent area of Halifax with large Victorian villas overlooking the seventy acres of common land that give the area its name. The open ground is known locally as 'the moor.' It was land acquired from the Savile family, historic landowners in the area, for £100 in 1866 to be set aside as recreational ground on condition that it 'remain unenclosed for perpetuity' and that 'the council do something about smoke abatement.' A refreshment lodge built on the edge of the park in the 1880s caused considerable local controversy but the needs of promenading Victorians won the day and, being discreetly positioned, it doesn't detract from the main area of grassland. It rises up the hill almost to a point with the former Crossley Orphanage which became the Crossley and Porter School and then the Crossley Heath School sitting at the top with long straight roads on the other three sides. It has a perimeter of around a mile which made it a perfect choice for loathsome cross-country runs in PE lessons whilst we were at the school.

Behind the grand villas with their pleasant outlook are rows of terraced houses of varying sizes, from back to backs to streets of much larger and grander terraced houses. At the very top of Free School Lane (named after the Heath Grammar School which was given its charter by Elizabeth I) and across the road from Crossley Heath is another area of open ground called Spring Edge. There, unattractive 1960s box housing replaced an area of densely packed terraces which had been in the shadow of the substantial Scarborough Mills which were still standing in the late 1980s. Although not mysteriously burning down like so many other vacant mills, it was finally demolished to be replaced by a Tesco. Savile Park had a very mixed housing stock where back to backs rubbed shoulders as neighbours with the much grander villas. Apparently at one point there was a plan to eradicate all the back to back housing in the town but luckily for us, the bulldozers didn't reach Savile Park which meant that a treasure was saved that generations have enjoyed and continue to do so.

The cluster of streets across from Crossley Heath School and Spring Edge that are Ingram Street, Horsfall Street and Thomas Street West are narrow streets of small back to back houses. Turning off Free School Lane into Ingram Street really did feel like stepping back in time. On Ingram Street, there were a few terraced houses and a small factory on the corner which was still operating at the time before later being converted into small flats. A sharp ninety degree turn at the end took you into Thomas Street West where, looking up the incline of the street, it just appeared to be an old world northern street, narrow and with small terraced houses on each side.

Somebody had told us that somewhere in these streets there was a great little pub that was worth going into. It was a bit of an old man's pub, whatever that meant, but they said it was worth a visit nonetheless. With it being just up the road from where we lived, we felt obliged to explore and so one night Bob and I headed up Free School Lane, took the right onto Ingram Street and then the left but looking up Thomas Street West we couldn't initially see anything that looked like a pub. It just looked like a street of houses to us. We then spotted an unlit sign, swinging lazily about halfway up the street. Perhaps this was the mysterious hidden pub people had talked about. We hadn't considered that we might be looking for a pub in the middle of a street. We walked up towards the sign and sure enough there was a pub there, sandwiched between the houses. We couldn't see anything inside because of the thick stained-glass windows and so we nervously pushed the door open and stepped into the fug of smoke and hum of conversation that so typified the place. We had found the Big Six and it was to be a revelation.

The Big Six is one of those places that hasn't changed and that is one of the reasons that so many people like it. It is small and cosy and still partitioned into its separate areas, looking the same as it would have done when some of its patrons first started going in there forty or fifty years previously. It was spared the character sapping rebuilding and re-modelling which so many pubs endured in the 1960s and 1970s when partitions were ripped down to create large open spaces. The tiny terraced houses on Thomas Street West are back to back and the street at the back of the pub is Horsfall Street, also made up of back to back houses. The Big Six's footprint reflects its origins in six back to back houses on Thomas Street West and Horsfall Street and the pub still is still laid out in three sections.

The Big Six was to become a fundamental part of our growing up. It retains a near mythological status, part of our shared heritage. It's a beautiful little pub that made such an impression on us as youngsters. A return to Halifax over the subsequent many years away was not complete without a visit where we would walk in the door, see that nothing has changed, see the same familiar faces who were always pleased to see us, have a couple of pints and then not go back again for several months when the same warm welcome and the same great beer was repeated.

It still prospers with whole new generations of customers who appreciate its charms as much as we were about to. It constantly attracts new devotees who love it as much as we do. It is such a cliché, but it really is the epitome of the friendly local community pub. You can start talking to strangers, or more often they start talking to you, within seconds of going in because whether you stand at the tiny bar or take a seat, you're never far away from anyone. You just can't hide away in a remote corner. It has an eclectic mix of regular customers now just like it did back then and we would spend our time sitting and chatting with the locals rather than hitting the town. We spent so many afternoons and evenings in there at a real character-forming time of our lives where we learned about pubs, beer and talking to adults from all walks of life. We learned about the pub as a real community meeting place, overseen by a long-standing landlord. We learned that the pub was a place where problems could be shared, sorrows drowned and good news celebrated. We learned that pubs can be full of diverse and interesting characters, as well as more than the occasional bore, and we loved every minute of it.

We were young chaps, sixth formers with our lives ahead of us. Perhaps we should have been in town unsuccessfully trying to talk to girls in nightclubs, but why on earth did we need to do that? We could go to the Big Six and drink amazing beer and play dominoes and chat with men that were, amongst other things, smelly, old and weird, but who were always welcoming and ready with a good anecdote. We talked to real pub characters who were as much a part of the pub as the bricks and mortar.

Different characters appeared at different times but we particularly enjoyed the lunchtime crowd during the school holidays. We even started creeping in on Friday lunchtimes because free periods followed Friday lunchtime once we moved into the upper sixth. Of course, with 'A' levels looming we should perhaps have been using that time a bit more productively, but as teenagers we knew best. We were learning some life experience instead.

We hadn't really settled on our preferred drink before discovering the Big Six. We had already experimented with Hofmeister and Miller Genuine Draft. I had tried Websters Green Label thinking that bitter was more 'traditional,' more 'Yorkshire,' more 'manly' than lager, plus Green Label was generally cheaper than regular bitter. It might even have been technically classed as a 'mild.' Our beer of choice was to be confirmed when we discovered the Big Six, a Tetley house, and we first tried their Tetley Bitter. After that first mouthful, we never looked back. It was an outstanding pint with a creamy head, coppery brown colour and a subtle, but distinct taste. It was neither bland nor overpowering, perfection in a glass. We instantly became bitter converts and devotees of Tetley. Although the Big Six was our favourite, Tetley pubs became our destinations of choice. We became very particular, some may even say boring, comparing pints between different pubs and turning our noses up if we were somewhere where Tetley was not available and we had to make do with something inferior.

Despite the amazing beers available these days, nothing will ever taste as good as the Tetley we drank in Halifax over the next four or five years. Some old timers in the town say that Tetley Bitter was nothing special in the 1960s. Back then it didn't have the same dominance in the town because there were still three good sized brewers in the town (Websters, Ramsdens and Whitakers), all brewing beer for their own pub estates. They claim that Tetley only improved when Ramsdens was acquired by Tetley (which was by then part of Allied Breweries) in the late 1960s. The Ramsdens brewery was promptly closed and demolished to make way for the enormous new headquarters of the Halifax Building Society. The expertise was allegedly spirited over to the Tetley brewery in Leeds and only then did Tetley Bitter improve. This is an unverified, anecdotal tale told to me, needless to say, in a pub.

We looked forward to every visit to the Big Six. Walking through the door on the Thomas Street West side there was an enormous cigarette machine on the wall on the left and often sat at the table underneath it would be one of the locals whose name I never knew despite him going in for years. He always sat on the same stool, I think with his own handled glass, and never said a word. He just kept himself to himself and then after a couple of pints he would return his glass to the bar with an ever so cheerful 'Cheerio!' He always acknowledged us when we went in but was never interested in engaging us in conversation. A good judge of character, some might say.

On the right, across from the cigarette machine was the 'games room,' though to call it a games room is stretching it a little. It was a small room with a couple of tables, some dominoes and a dart board which, given that the room was so small, could only be used to play darts if you were the only people in there. Crazy kids that we were, we often sat in the games room on Friday nights for a game of dominoes. This room had lino on the floor, a gas fire and more basic furniture. On the other side of the dividing wall with 'Big Six' in stained glass was the lounge. This was an equally small room except, being the lounge, it had carpet, an open fire and comfier seats. There were still the buzzers around the wall from the days of table service in pub lounges. Walking straight through the pub without going into the games room or the lounge would take you past the fruit machines to a door opposite the entrance we came in and an exit onto Horsfall Street.

Going past the games room and turning left past the cigarette machine took you to the middle section of the pub where the bar was, hidden from sight on entering through either door. The bar itself is tiny, barely six feet in length and only a couple of feet deep. Most of the glasses are on a shelf above the bar or kept in crates in the back room because there was hardly any room to store anything. The compacted nature of the bar and the low shelf meant that anyone behind the bar seemed to be almost peering out of a mass of wood, pumps, and glass.

Peering out from behind the cramped bar in 1988 were the husband and wife team of Duncan and Sheila who had run the pub for years. Duncan was a bit of a misery guts, frequently looking as if he'd just got out of bed, but he was always alright with us, whereas Sheila was much friendlier. The bar counter itself wasn't too crowded given that back then only Tetley and, later, Burton Ale were the only two hand-pulled beers on sale. Burton Ale wasn't anywhere near as popular as the Tetley, but we did try it occasionally until we finally learned the perils of the 'Burton head' the next day.

We would order our Tetley and then move to the left to sit in our favourite spot, the snug. The snug was where our real Big Six experience was to be during that final year of school. It consisted of two small bench seats, a couple of small tables and a few stools. More stools were often brought in and people squeezed around the tables making it very cosy at times, but not so much when were in at lunchtime. On our lunchtime visits the snug regulars had the bench seats and we were relegated to the stools. Sitting down with our pints we would then entertained by old men sparking off each other and sharing stories and gossip and it was fascinating to listen to. They went to the pub for the company as much as the beer and having a new audience who would listen to their tales was a breath of fresh air for them. They liked talking and we liked listening.

There was a small group of snug regulars when we started going in. We always sat in the snug on the left but at the opposite side under the window looking on to Horsfall Street was a much smaller snug, basically a corner seat that you could sit on the end of and place your pint on the bar. The bar area was small enough for conversation to take place between the two snugs without having to raise your voice. Whilst the left snug had its regular occupants, there was an infrequent visitor in those early days who spent his lunchtimes in the Big Six when he was around. He seemed ever so glamorous to us because he was an engineer working in Indonesia. He was a bit more aloof than the others in the lunchtime crowd and dipped in and out of conversation, but his tales of life in the Far East and his seemingly dazzling intelligence made him quite a fascinating character. He would sit on the end seat, skinny legs crossed, sipping halves of Tetley with whisky chasers, a folded *Daily Telegraph* on his lap, effortlessly switching between anecdote and rapid completion of clues in the cryptic crossword. Then he would disappear for a couple of months, only for us to wander in and find him there again with his half of Tetley, a chaser, his crossword and more tales of life in Asia.

Interesting as he was, he came and went whereas the legendary snug regulars that made our early days in the Big Six so enjoyable were the quartet of the left snug drinkers. There was 'Bendy Fred,' an odd and very quiet man who didn't say very much. He seemed quite content just listening and laughing, chipping in with the occasional comment. Still to this day we have no idea where he got the name Bendy from. The only thing I can think is that it was because he sat very slumped on the bench, so much so that I was surprised he never slid off the freshly polished faux leather.

Apart from Bendy Fred were fellow senior citizens Harold and Edgar and the much younger caretaker from our school across the road, Michael. Edgar was an elderly chap who, unlike the slow drinking Bendy Fred really did put his beer away. He was a real old school Yorkshireman, probably well into his sixties with a cloth cap perched on the top of his head, dirty boots, scruffy pants and a jumper clinging tightly to his substantial beer belly. He'd sink a few pints at lunchtime then maybe wander on somewhere else after the Big Six closed for a couple of hours in the afternoon before a few more at home. We were quite impressed at the time that a man of his age could consume beer like he did.

Like plenty of others of his generation sitting in pubs, it didn't take him long to get talking about 'the good old days' and, inevitably, the war. Unlike so many other old men in pubs telling daring and hugely far-fetched stories of how they single-handedly re-captured France after D-Day, Edgar told us that he was a conscientious objector and was very open about it. It may have been a shaggy dog story, but one of the more memorable tales that he told us was that as a young man called up to non-combat duties, one of his tasks was to take part in flights over occupied Norway to drop propaganda leaflets. He described enduring long, dark, cold, terrifying flights on rickety planes with no machine gun turrets to defend them if they were intercepted. Being shot down would mean certain death in the freezing cold North Sea.

Once over Norway and at the designated drop zone his job was to open the door and throw the leaflets out of the plane before turning around and getting back to England as quickly as possible, thankful to still be alive. On one of the flights he got an assistant, another conscientious objector. Over Norway the call came to offload and the door was opened. Edgar got to work to jettison the leaflets as quickly as possible in to the chilly night air from an extremely dangerous position standing by the open door of a plane several thousand feet above Norway with minimal safety precautions. Once the door was shut and they were no longer clinging on for dear life and could hear each other again, his new colleague looked at him incredulously, dumbstruck at what he had just seen. When he had composed himself, he asked Edgar if it had been pointed out to him in his briefing that he was supposed to take the leaflets out of the boxes before throwing them out of the plane. Oh, how we laughed.

Harold was another elderly war veteran who liked a lunchtime drink of Tetley with an occasional whisky chaser. He was a charming old man, very polite and always well dressed. He would wander in on his own and wasn't too precious about where he sat, switching between different sides of the snug depending who was in and how much space there was. He was quite happy to chat, but also happy to listen, just enjoying the buzz and conversation going on around him. He looked close to death when we first met him with a shuffling walk, severe curvature of the spine and pink, sore looking dry skin making him look far older than he was. It turned out his diet was shocking and consisted mainly of a trip into town most days for a big fry up followed by drinks at lunchtime and then maybe a couple more if he wandered up at night. A few changes to his diet and the introduction of a bit of fruit seemed to make the world of difference and he kept going for years and years, to the point where the subsequent landlord would drive down to pick him up and bring him to the pub because he was too frail to make the journey on his own. Still always well dressed, he would sit quietly for an hour or two enjoying the buzz of the pub and maybe a couple of half pints. He became a kind of elder statesman of the pub, the last of that old generation that had drunk there for years. The landlord would then drive him back home and make sure he got back in to his house safely, but those days were a long way away at this point. He was ex-RAF but he never talked about the war or what he did. He carried around a picture of an extremely dashing younger Harold in his uniform with an attractive woman on his arm but, like his war stories, he was gentlemanly and discreet and never elaborated.

Bringing the average age of the group down was the final member of the group. Michael was the caretaker at our school just across the road and he spent his lunchtimes having a long liquid and cigarette based lunch. He claimed he could do this because he was up so early getting the school ready in the morning and he would then be working late finding it better, he claimed, to get things done after the kids had gone. Whether that was true or not I have no idea but he was certainly very different and more dynamic than the former caretaker who was a thin, old, balding chap in a traditional brown smock and as he got closer and closer to retirement seemed to spend an awful lot of time checking the boiler room with his pipe and a box of Swan Vestas.

Michael really liked to talk. He was very articulate and he liked an audience and we liked his anecdotes. Some of them seemed more than a little far-fetched but they were good tales regardless. He certainly did seem to take a shine to us. Many of his stories stemmed from his time in the Merchant Navy and his worldwide travels and whether they were the truth, extensions of the truth or fiction didn't really matter because they were all cracking stories. After numerous pints, he would then wander back across to the school, *Daily Telegraph* under his arm, probably to inspect the boiler. We never saw him in the pub in the evenings but he did call in at weekend lunchtimes, this time scrubbed up and smartly dressed rather than in his boiler suit, sitting in the same spot with his *Telegraph* for a longer session given that he wasn't going back to work.

It was fascinating to be part of their little circle and listen to these tales of distant lands and local gossip None of them were bothered that we were under-age or even that we perhaps should have been at school. Our futures were to be determined by the looming exams, not by having a cheeky Friday or Sunday lunchtime pint. Michael always offered plenty of encouragement about our exams and the big wide world out there that could open up for us if we did well in them.

As the Spring of 1989 arrived Bob and I were both legal Big Six drinkers, familiar faces in the snug and facing our 'A' levels. Our last day at school in May was notable for being a baking hot day that got increasingly hot and humid during the afternoon before breaking with an apocalyptic thunderstorm at tea-time that caused flooding in the town centre despite it being on a hill and washed away bridges in local beauty spots. Luckily the storm didn't arrive until after the long-practised tradition of the upper sixth form heading to the Big Six for an afternoon of drinking on their last day at school. The pub was empty apart from a couple of dozen drunken sixth formers (and Michael) and it wasn't exactly subtle given that we were all in our school uniform. It was a tradition that had gone on for years and carried on long after we left. School was behind us and I never again saw most of the people that were there. I was glad to be out of the place (the school that is, not the Big Six).

There was one legacy of that final day of school in the Big Six that has lasted an astonishing near thirty years in the pub. The Big Six has its fair share of bric-a-brac high on a shelf running around the pub. The usual things are there, plates, old bottles and the like. Though the circumstances of quite how it came to be there are a little hazy, somehow Bob donated his sixth form tie to the collection. Sheila hung it at the back of the bar and amazingly it is still there in exactly the same place. The original grey is barely recognizable, replaced with nicotine brown and it resembles a piece of cardboard rather than a tie, but it is still there and is the kind of touch that endears us to the pub. At the Big Six, things never change - and that's what makes it so special.

6 WORKING IN PUBS - 1

I couldn't blame it on drinking beer in the Big Six. It wasn't the occasional pint in the Big Six that made me screw up my 'A' levels. Laziness and complacency had far more to do with it. The fateful results day in August 1989 revealed that I wouldn't be going to university along with just about everyone else from sixth form, including Bob. Unlike me, he had realised just how little work he had done over the previous two years with all our distractions and he knuckled down intensively, effectively dropping out of school for the last couple of weeks to cram in two years of work and secure fabulous results. He was off on his adventures and I was to remain in Halifax with no one to go to the Big Six with and no idea what I was going to do. Unbelievably, I was to barely go in to the Big Six again for nearly two years.

I had started the year drinking gorgeous pints of Tetley in the Big Six and I had been hoping to be ending it drinking cheap beer out of plastic glasses at some polytechnic Student Union whilst studying town and country planning. I had done the rounds of visits in places like Birmingham (grim), Oxford (nice) and Dundee (cold). It wasn't to be and I was ending the year working in a paper recycling factory where I spent several weeks emptying bag after bag of office paper into a giant shredder and re-bagging the shreds. It was a valuable life lesson because, bad results or not, I knew it would be temporary. The lads I was working with didn't have that luxury. It was relatively short-lived because towards the end of the year I managed to get a job in the head office of the Halifax Building Society on the site of the old Ramsdens brewery.

Bob had disappeared on his gap year and just as I was discovering my enjoyment of pubs and Tetley beer the visits were brought to an abrupt end. Little did I appreciate it at the time, but the pub environment that we were just getting familiar with was about to start changing dramatically.

42

When scanning the photographs I mentioned earlier, I found a headline that I had cut from *The Times*. As we were regular Big Six visitors at the time, the front-page headline made us chuckle as the paper announced, 'Young set to break Big Six beer monopoly.'

Obviously, this wasn't our Big Six but the large brewers that had emerged from the acquisitions and mergers of the 1950s and 1960s when smaller breweries and their pub estates were taken over, frequently closed and the acquired pubs were rebranded and started selling the new owner's products. These activities, which continued throughout the 1970s, had resulted in a situation where by the 1980s the 'Big Six' brewery groups owned over 70% of British beer production and around 70% of pubs through the tied-house system in which beer was sold. Put simply, the Big Six pub was a Tetley house and therefore sold only Tetley products. Except for the very few free houses that were around, if you preferred a certain beer you had to go to one of their pubs or put up with the limited choice in the tied-house pub you had chosen.

In the late 1980s as we started exploring pubs in Halifax, there were only two main choices in the town. We generally headed to Tetley pubs to drink our favourite beer that was brewed at the Hunslet brewery in Leeds, fifteen miles to the east. There were hundreds, if not thousands, of Tetley houses around Yorkshire by the late 1980s. Through mergers and takeovers Tetley had built up a massive pub estate from its humble origins in 1822. For many years, it was one of numerous relatively modest regional breweries in Yorkshire, and one of several brewers in Leeds. In 1960, there was a cross-Pennine merger with Walker Cain of Warrington to create Tetley-Walker with an estate of three thousand pubs. A subsequent merger with Ansells of Birmingham and Ind Coope of Burton created Allied Breweries which in turn merged with food group J Lyons to create Allied Lyons.

Most other pubs in the town were owned by Websters. After the local Ramsdens and Whitakers breweries had been taken over and closed in the late 1960s by Allied Breweries and Whitbread respectively, Websters remained the sole brewer in the town. It had been brewing since 1838 at the Fountain Head brewery in a picturesque valley a couple of miles outside the town. Like Crossleys' Carpets, the Halifax Building Society and Mackintosh's (the company that gave the world Quality Street and now owned by Nestle) they were a significant local employer and were another proud national brand for a small town. Their main brand at the time was Websters Yorkshire Bitter which received great exposure and increased sales through the timely shirt sponsorship of Halifax RLFC just in time for their magnificent run to victory in the 1987 rugby league Challenge Cup final at Wembley. We were never fans of Websters. It tasted bland and watery and nowhere near as good as Tetley.

When we were discovering beer, Websters was no longer an independent local brewery. It failed to escape the clutches of larger concerns and it was acquired by London brewery Watney Mann in 1972. Grand Metropolitan took over Watney Mann later that year but unlike many less fortunate breweries, it remained open and the brands were retained. Websters was then merged with Wilsons of Manchester in 1985. Other breweries were represented in the town but in much smaller numbers of pubs. There were a few Whitbread houses and it was possible to drink beer from Sheffield's Wards, Sunderland's Vaux, Tadcaster's Samuel Smiths and Burton's Bass.

The dominance of the big brewery groups didn't escape the attention of campaigners and interfering politicians as well as frustrated independent brewers struggling to get their products into pubs. The six breweries were Allied Breweries, Bass Carrington, Courage Imperial, Scottish and Newcastle, Watney and Whitbread. The Monopolies and Mergers Commission got involved in 1986 and three years later came *The Times'* headline heralding the infamous 1989 'Beer Orders.' The Commission said the long-standing tied-house system that was common around the country was the main offender because it restricted customer choice by only allowing their beers to be sold. The Beer Orders decreed that brewers owning more than two thousand tied houses were to dispose of the surplus in excess of two thousand by 31st October 1992. In addition, from May 1990 remaining brewery tied houses were to stock a guest ale from another brewery and they would also be able to buy other drinks from producers outside of the tie. Change was coming but we were oblivious to it. We weren't bothered about choice when there was Tetley on the bar.

So, fast forward from the Beer Orders to the spring of 1991 via an almost pub free year in 1990. Bob had returned from his gap year and was at university, coming home for a Big Six catch up at the end of each term. On the surface, nothing much seemed to have changed. Tetley still owned pubs and were still selling their beer in them and Websters were still selling their beer in theirs. The town remained dominated by the two breweries.

I was working in my office and barely going to the pub and those early days in the Big Six were becoming a distant memory. Work was going well, but I was getting restless. After finally heading off to the Midlands to see Bob in his university, I impulsively decided that university was for me. Despite the sudden decision, March was not the best time to start thinking about going because it was far too late to enter the process to start in the upcoming September. Undeterred, and in a rare instance of forward planning, I started to think ahead to September 1992.

It just seemed the right thing to do. Admittedly my exposure to university life that weekend had been at one of the best universities in the country but the whole lifestyle appealed to me. People were having a wonderful time as students without the daily routine of work. There would be plenty of time to be sat in an office and I was already seeing graduate trainees only a couple of years older than me being parachuted into the company at a much higher level by-passing the multiple rungs on the ladder that I would have to painfully climb one by one. I quite enjoyed my job and was reasonably competent. My boss was encouraging me to study for professional qualifications and I reasoned that if I was going to study for a professional qualification that was at near degree level then I might as well move away from home, get a degree and hopefully have a lot of fun in the process. I wasn't motivated by money which was good considering my pitiful salary and so I didn't think that being an impoverished student would be too much of a hardship. The 2% staff mortgage rate was a great perk in the days when interest rates were more than 10%, but it wasn't sufficient motivation to stay because buying a house didn't feature in my plans even with the bargain basement property prices in Halifax at the time. It didn't take long to make the decision to pack it all in but with my terrible 'A' level results I just needed to persuade somewhere to accept me onto a course on the strength of my work experience.

I also needed to be patient. Assuming I could get a place, I wouldn't be starting for almost eighteen months which at the time seemed a long, long way away. There was no need to worry, though, because that time was about to fly by. That early Summer of 1991 was to see a long overdue re-acquaintance with Tetley. Bob returned from his gap year and his first year at university to spend the Summer holidays back in Halifax for the first time since we left school two years previously. He had picked up some work at our old Saturday night pre-Crossleys' Bar pit stop, the Brass Cat. It was still a popular place and was still well run, still bright and airy and it still sold great Tetley.

With the plans for applying to university in place as soon as the application window opened, Bob persuaded me to get some part time bar work saying that it would be a valuable skill to have if I was needing work when I became a student. I also had a lot of time on my hands because I didn't do much in the evenings and at weekends. Bar work was something I hadn't really thought of and even if I had I wouldn't have known where to start having already been burned by my Hobbit experience a few years earlier. Luckily, with working at the Brass Cat Bob knew plenty of people in the local Tetley community and recommended me to another town centre Tetley landlord from unfamiliar territory.

His name was Andy and he ran the nearby Portman and Pickles which was a pub we had only very occasionally gone in to. It attracted more of a student and alternative crowd, lots of leather jackets and loud rock music, especially at the weekend. Andy just happened to be in the courtyard at the back of the Brass Cat one evening and after being introduced and having a brief chat he said to come down to the pub the night after for another chat. It was a conversation that was to change my relationship with pubs and beer forever.

The Portman and Pickles, known locally as the Portman, was run by Andy and his wife Mandy. Bob and I had met them a couple of years previously when they managed the Westgate, a smaller and quieter Tetley pub just a short walk from the Portman near the entrance to the Piece Hall. It was seemingly the training pub for Tetley's managers in the town before they went on to manage one of the larger pubs with several local landlords starting their careers there. He had seemed a pleasant enough bloke, though he was usually very drunk on our occasional visits. He remained in the memory for a long time after a night when he challenged us to play pool and then used his astonishingly putrid flatulence as part of his tactics to put us off. It's strange how things like that stay with you and, needless to say, I didn't remind him of that when we met the next night. A short chat later and that was that, he took me on and I was a bar man. Well, a bar man on trial at least. I was to come in for a shift on a quiet Tuesday night to see how I got on.

The Tuesday arrived and my dad gave me a lift into town, a little nervous about where I was starting work. It was a pub that seemingly had a bit of a 'reputation' as they say, especially amongst those with memories going back to the late 1960s. It was a decent sized pub with acres of living space above it. It had an elegant Victorian façade and had been incorporated into the impressive Borough Market that had opened in 1896. It wasn't the Portman then and was known by its original name, the Wheatsheaf, for many years. Various people I have spoken to remember it as being a place to avoid in its days as the Wheatsheaf. There was all manner of stories about its use by local prostitutes and of fearsome lock-ins where customers were literally locked in and expected to drink and spend money into the early hours. How much of this is true I don't know for sure and Andy, who told us some of these stories, was prone to occasional exaggeration. Over the years though, conversations in other pubs around the town with people old enough to remember it all tell tales and rumours along similar lines. It was a place that many avoided, that was for sure. Plenty of people, my parents included, were horrified when I said I was working there even though it hadn't been the Wheatsheaf for over twenty years.

Its past life as the Wheatsheaf can be seen by looking up at the building from Market Street where a sheaf of wheat can be seen carved into the stone of the increasingly tatty-looking building. Its reputation may have prompted a name change and a revamp and, showing that re-naming pubs is nothing new, it changed from being the Wheatsheaf to become the William Dighton in the late 1960s. William Dighton secured his place in the history of the town by being murdered. He was an excise inspector who set out to end the widespread 18th century practice of 'coining' and to bring down the notorious and very successful Cragg Vale 'coiners.' Cragg Vale was a remote valley several miles from Halifax heading in to the Pennine moors. The gang based there clipped the edge of gold coins and carefully collected the clippings. It was then melted down and new gold coins were struck using illegally made dies. The gang's sophistication, as well as the remote location and difficult terrain made their capture especially difficult given the law and order resources available at the time.

Dighton didn't give up in his quest to close down the gang and, with the assistance of informers, he arrested the ringleader, 'King' David Hartley who was imprisoned in York Castle and subsequently hanged. This had severe consequences for Dighton. The rest of the gang were determined to carry on their illegal trade and they also wanted revenge. Hartley's brother arranged for Dighton to be killed and he was shot dead outside his Halifax home in 1769. The perpetrators were caught and suffered a particularly gruesome end in York. Their bodies were brought back to the town and hung from a gibbet on Beacon Hill with their arm outstretched pointing to the scene of the crime to supposedly deter other criminals.

Gibbets were structures on which criminals were hung, often in a cage, dead or sometimes alive, to deter others. To confuse things, Halifax was notorious for having another gibbet which was an early guillotine-style device with a heavy axe head used to decapitate criminals convicted of minor offences. Ancient tradition gave rights to the Lord of the Manor of Wakefield to issue justice in this way and theft of goods over the value of 13½d was sufficient to warrant execution. Although decapitation had been a common punishment with the earliest recorded occasion being in 1286, the construction of a device for the task and the length of time it was used for made the town unusual. It was used for the last time in 1650 after over fifty known executions and Oliver Cromwell later ended 'Halifax Gibbet Law.' Gibbet Street passes the site which was neglected until rediscovered during construction work around 1840 and a replica gibbet was built in 1974. The Running Man pub, lower down the hill on Pellon Lane, recognises the two men who successfully managed to escape to the boundary of the Forest of Hardwick which made them free men. One man was never seen again. The other returned after several years, perhaps thinking things would have blown over. They hadn't, and he lost his head.

Despite organising the murder, Hartley's brother was never reprimanded and he lived a long and free life though Dighton's murder, and the overwhelming response from the authorities, did signal the beginning of the end of illicit coining.

Change at the pub came again in the late 1980s when it was refurbished and renamed with more local connections, thankfully neither of whom were murdered. Eric Portman was an early star of black and white films from the 1930s until just before his death in 1969. He had been born in Boothtown, not far from the pub just outside the town centre. Wilfred Pickles was also from the town and made his name as an actor and radio presenter over the same period.

We had very rarely gone into the Portman before I started working there. Going in through the main door on Market Street there was a small room to the right with a tiled floor dominated by a pool table and it was the only part of the pub that had any natural light. Walking straight ahead from the entrance there was a short corridor and then a couple of low steps which led to the main bar area which went deep into the building. On the right was a long bar which met a pillar at the far end before continuing around the corner for a short length, giving the pub an 'L' shaped floor-space. At the far end of the pub and directly opposite but unseen from the main entrance at the front was a small rear door which led into a dark passageway which exited into the covered Victorian arcade outside one of the entrances to the Borough Market.

This lack of natural light, dark furniture and maroon and brown themed décor gave the place something of a gloomy feel. It was very easy to lose track of what time of day it was, making it feel very isolated from the outside world.

Like many other pubs in the town at the time, the weekends were very lively but, for a town centre pub, it also had very much of a 'local' feel. There were several small communities of regulars who would come in for a few drinks after work or shopping and treated it very much as their local pub, even though many of them had to then get a bus home. There were also plenty of regulars who shuffled around the various Tetley pubs in the town on an evening being fans of the beer. They would move between the Portman, the Westgate, the Brass Cat and the Upper George, all decent pubs with great beer within a short walking distance.

I nervously went into the pub, which luckily for me on my first night working was very quiet. I found Andy and he proceeded to give a me a whistle-stop tour of the bar. There was only Tetley Bitter on the bar, regardless of the Beer Orders, as well as three lagers, two ciders and Guinness. It was a basic offering and standard for the time in tied-house pubs. White wine was served from a tap on the bar rather than from a bottle and I had to learn what a white wine spritzer was and how to make one, such was my ignorance. Wine was hardly ever requested by the glass given the poor reputation of pub wine at the time, especially in a rough and ready 'beer pub' like the Portman. We didn't even sell red wine.

Behind the bar there was a basic range of spirits which didn't sell particularly well apart from the vodka and, bizarrely, Pernod. Much as I was to later discover the pleasures of a pastis (Ricard or Pernod with water), at the time Pernod and blackcurrant was still a surprisingly popular drink. There were the mixers, soft drinks, a few bottles including Mackeson Stout and Gold Label barley wine, plus what turned out to be Andy's favourite tipple, canned Castlemaine XXXX. There was a lot to take in but it was the complicated looking itemised till that was the most awkward thing to grasp. After that, it was time to learn how to pull a pint of Tetley properly. I didn't really have any idea how the beer I had been drinking was served or appreciated the skill and technique involved in pulling a pint. It is a straightforward task to do it right, but it can be easily messed up and the whole consistency of the pint can be ruined. The Tetley we had been drinking in the Big Six and a few places around the town was always good because the landlords had exacting standards, looked after their cellars properly and trained their staff right to do it right. Plus, customers knew what they wanted and what to expect. I wasn't very well travelled at the time and so I was unable to compare the Tetley experience with elsewhere. However, I was soon to realise the importance of the small plastic attachment called the sparkler. This was what made the Tetley, and other northern beers, so delicious. The consistency of the beer was transformed by the sparkler which was screwed onto the end of the metal serving pipe every day and removed and cleaned at night. The sparkler 'agitated' the beer as it was pulled through, giving the beer a wonderful, creamy consistency, which settled into a head on the top of the pint, rather than being served flat, headless and boring like pints served 'down south' where sparklers were rarely used.

To get that traditional northern pint, the glass was placed right under the serving pipe with the sparkler touching the centre of the bottom the glass. The pump handle on the bar was gripped firmly followed by an initial sharp pull to get the beer agitated through the sparkler and then in one continuous movement the pump was slowly and steadily pulled to its full extent, around forty-five degrees. This first movement delivered half a pint of creamy Tetley into the glass. The pump handle was then returned to a fully upright position before the second pull was started. This was a slower but still steady pull to deliver the second half. As the glass was getting almost full, it was slowly lowered and the pipe removed just as the glass was full to the brim. The pint was then left to settle whilst taking payment or preparing other drinks. In the time it takes to sort out the cash in the till or whilst another pint is being poured, the beer should have settled and if it was done properly it should only require a minimal top up, if it needed one at all.

The pumps at the Portman worked perfectly for a two-pull pint. After satisfactorily delivering my pint, albeit a little slowly, Andy was happy. He said he preferred people with no experience because they didn't bring any bad habits (little did he know) and he hung around for an hour or so as I got through my first customers. He seemed happy enough because at the end of the night he allocated me what would be my regular shifts which were to be Tuesday night and Friday night. He also asked me to cover the

Saturday afternoon and night shift that coming weekend. It was supposed to be a one-off but I became a permanent fixture.

Evenings during the week weren't particularly busy, but they were always 'steady.' There may have been an occasional rush, but generally there was always time to keep on top of things, collect and wash the glasses and keep the place looking tidy. There was also time to chat to the regulars, many of whom were good fun and really liked interacting with the bar staff, making them feel more at home in their local. There were plenty who weren't bothered and kept themselves to themselves and plenty who just moaned at you about how much they had lost at the bookies or how life was giving them yet another kicking. It was depressing listening but they just wanted someone to talk to. There were those who spent their days drinking away their pension shuffling between pubs and bookmakers with their carrier bags from the discounted food shops around the town. Thankfully there were one or two who were real 'characters,' good fun with entertainment always guaranteed when they came in.

Overwhelmingly though, the weekday regulars were good, loyal, decent customers who enjoyed coming in, liked to be looked after and felt part of the pub. The pub was important to them and they clearly hadn't had the advantages that I had already had in life and they just wanted to have a few drinks, feel looked after and have a bit of a laugh before they headed home. This was far easier to do during the week when it was quieter and you could spend more time chatting and interacting with them. They were happy to buy you a drink every now and again if you looked after them and their generosity encouraged us to do so. After all, free beer is the best kind of beer.

I was too young and naive at the time to be aware of problem drinkers. To me, going to the pub was all about having a few beers and enjoying yourself. Many of these regulars were clearly heavy, sometimes very heavy, drinkers. I thought nothing of it at the time but there were some who I would meet later in life looking ravaged after years of very unhealthy living of which heavy drinking was a major part. Many of the weekday regulars opened up to the staff after some time and many of them had hard lives, money worries, dull jobs, no jobs, chaotic home lives or strained family and other relationships. They got a lot of mutual support from each other and a sense of community from meeting in the Portman for a few drinks. They were decent people, always nice to the staff, and the Portman meant a lot to them. They would come in, see who was in and enjoy a laugh or a moan together before they trudged off to the bus station and home to the varying parts of town where they lived.

The weekends brought a very different and a much, much bigger crowd into the pub. There were still plenty of the Tetley loving regulars but they had to jostle for space on Friday and Saturday nights with the young weekend crowd. It was popular with students and more 'alternative' types. There were lots of Doc Martin boots, cardigans, dark make-up and leather jackets and it was a young, fun vibe. The Portman was part of the 'bottom of town' circuit of more 'grungy' pubs at the weekend with lots of guitar music on the jukebox. The 'top of town' circuit was the opposite and was a more smartly dressed crowd although there was occasional overlap.

Some people would settle for the evening, but to do that you needed to get in early and commit to staying because as soon as you left your seat, it would be gone. Most people drifted around the 'circuit' going to pubs like the Upper George and the Union Cross and The Sportsman.

Whilst the Friday night crush didn't start to build until the early evening, on Saturdays it was busy from not long after opening. There was a regular and sizeable daytime drinking crowd who would be there all afternoon, shoppers would pop in and out and then at the end of Saturday afternoons a lot of traders from the Borough Market backing on to the pub would come in as well as staff from nearby shops. Staff from the long gone iconic Bradley's Records were regulars as were the much more pleasing on the eye girls from Boots across the road.

Many of the regular weekday crowd would also be in on Saturdays during the afternoon but they would drift off in the early evening when it got busier because they didn't like the crowds and didn't feel that it was 'their' pub when they didn't get the attention that they did during the week. It wasn't that they were being ignored, it was just that it was too busy to give them the time to chat that they would have had on a quieter day.

During the week, there would be a few that came in every single night, usually straight from work and who would then stay late sinking a *lot* of beer. It could easily be eight, nine or ten pints during an evening and that, to them, was quite normal. At the weekend, they would have a 'proper' drink, getting their seats not long after midday and they would still be there eight or nine hours later.

There was Stuart, a big jovial fellow with an enormous beer belly who, to us at least, genuinely seemed to enjoy his beer and being in the pub. He always had a smile and enjoyed a chat with the staff. He appreciated us even more when we discovered that he preferred the little used barrel glasses that modern-day hipsters seem to have discovered for themselves. A pint would easily disappear from these barrels in three or four gulps and it was a challenge to have enough fresh glasses for him as his consumption always out-paced cycles of the glass-washing machine. He was happy – preferred in fact - for his empty glass to be re-used for his next pint without washing it which horrified us. It would mean all the head that had remained clinging to the side of the glass being mixed in with a new pint swishing around the serving pipe which would go into everyone else's pint. Reusing glasses was quite standard at the time and is a horrible thought. The auto-vac system was popular where beer that overflowed from a glass when being poured was collected in a tray, but due to a vacuum it would be sucked out of the tray and back in to the pipe when the pump was next pulled, going into the next drink. It certainly helped with waste but if glasses were reused all that head from the previous pint would overflow into the tray and into the next glass. Hand hygiene was also important in that system given that beer that overflowed would run over your hand and into the tray. It's a great system and still in use in plenty of pubs, hopefully with clean glasses every time.

Stuart would hold court in the seating area across from the bar along with his sour-faced mate Dave, a heavy smoking miserable postal worker. He seemed to be the complete opposite personality type to Stuart, but he shared with him a fondness for a lot of Tetley every evening. Stuart was like a father figure to many of the regulars, especially some of the troubled, battle-hardened middle-aged women that used to come in. They would have a moan and a gripe to him and he always had an ear and a kind word for them. When his companions had called it a night and headed off home, Stuart would then wander up to the Brass Cat to see who was there and have a few more. He was always still going when everyone else had finished. He had an enormous capacity for beer though he looked far from a picture of health and I doubt his liver would have been very appreciative of what he was doing to it. I often wonder what happened to him.

With this new life in the Portman, my routine got quite busy. I was at the office on Monday to Friday from 8.30am until around 5pm and quite often later. Then it was home for some tea and on Wednesday and Friday evenings it would be the mile or so back into town to start work for 7pm. On weekday shifts, we'd be all finished and cleaned up for about 11.30pm but on Fridays we wouldn't be finished until at least midnight. We'd then have a drink and a chat rather than dashing off home and I would then be back in at 3pm on Saturday afternoon working a double shift straight through until closing. On Saturday nights, we would usually go out somewhere or do something afterwards, not getting home until the early hours. It was a sixty-hour working week and thanks to the invincibility of youth, I didn't even flinch.

With the weekend crush, it didn't take long for the place to be full. It wasn't a massive pub, but it certainly wasn't small and at peak periods there were a lot of people squashed in. It was often a jostle from the back entrance through which most people entered from other pubs in town to get to the bar. It was a busy, bustling pub on weekend evenings at the end of 1991 and the video jukebox was on constant play with endless repeats of Metallica's *Enter Sandman*, Black Crowes' *Hard to Handle* and Red Hot Chili Peppers' *Give It Away*.

It was a long bar, and it needed to be for us to cope with the volume of customers we were serving. On a weekend evening five of us would work relentlessly in the relatively cramped space pouring pint after pint. It was busy, but there was a lot of fun as well. When it is hot, sweaty, smoky and hectic, there is not much point in being there if you're not prepared to get into the spirit of things. There was always plenty of banter and joking around. If you didn't lighten up and join in, it would be a long, hard grind. Regular chest infections soon became a regular workplace hazard, but I still disagreed with the smoking ban. I wanted to work there and pubs aren't health clubs after all.

The staff were as eclectic as the customers which added to the enjoyment of working there. Everyone was different. The regular staff included a computer programmer by day who was also a gym freak and partial to turning up to work in a skimpy vest to show off his physique to impress the women he rarely spoke to. There was a long-haired rocker with a good line in banter who did speak to lots of women but rarely with the result he was hoping for. There was a narrowboat dwelling hippy with bright clothes and long hair and we were all supposedly supervised by a Geordie cellar man who, when he wasn't working in the pub was invariably drinking in one.

Despite being contrasting individuals with very different backgrounds, we all got on as a team to do what needed to be done and we did it in an enjoyable way. On the hectic weekend evenings, a busy pub just won't function without teamwork because any shirking or not doing what was needed to be done would mean that everyone else had to work harder. Being a predominantly all-male staff also meant that there was lots of testosterone and a competitive spirit. Those not up to scratch were soon weeded out.

I managed to hold down the two jobs with ease. Heading into October and November the Portman became my whole social life as well as a source of a few extra pounds, both financial and physical with the increased beer intake and the discovery of post-drinking curries and kebabs. I was working there three nights a week and most of Saturday. My applications to universities and polytechnics were submitted and I just had to wait for news. Although the dismal 'A' levels were becoming a distant memory I was confident that my office days were numbered and the experience I had gained at work was going to get me on to a course. Things were going well at the Portman and then in the run up to Christmas 1991, they got so much better.

I had barely known Bob's older brother Phil in all the time we had been friends which by then had been over five years. He was two years older and had been away at college for much of that time and rarely around. After graduating that year with a degree in which he had no interest which trained him for a career in which he had even less interest in an industry that at the time was in the doldrums (and in which he also had no interest), by the Autumn he was unemployed at home in Halifax and getting in his parents' way.

One Friday night I was due to go to my office Christmas party, that annual chore of office life when an overpriced turkey dinner, a crappy disco and drink-fuelled tears were, rather bizarrely, looked forward to by many. When the rota for that week was pinned on the noticeboard I was down to work despite supposedly booking the Friday night off. I wasn't that bothered about going but I had paid my money and got on well with my colleagues. I asked Bob who was back from university for the Christmas holidays, but he couldn't help because he had already picked up work at the Brass Cat. News of my predicament soon reached Savile Park and Phil, who had himself done some time working behind bars in the past, including at the Brass Cat in its very early days, was given a non-negotiable ultimatum by his mother and was grudgingly commandeered into working my shift for me.

The Christmas party was unremarkable and expensive, as they generally are, and at the Portman Phil had settled in quickly, got on with it and put in a solid shift that had passed without incident. He was a sociable chap, very competent behind a bar and had got on well with the Portman team. After all the clearing up and getting ready for the next day had been done, Andy would generally make an appearance. He would normally be quite refreshed by this stage and he would hold court for a while whilst staff relaxed after a busy night with a drink whilst waiting for taxis home or deciding what they were going to do next.

On the night of Phil's guest stint, for some reason Andy suggested a game of poker to the assorted staff and the chosen few who had stayed behind. Andy had plenty of good characteristics when he was sober. From what I knew of him, which admittedly wasn't that much, he seemed to be a generally decent bloke, a loving husband and a proud father. However, as seemed to be the trend amongst many town centre pub managers at the time, they were not known for putting time in behind the bars of their own pubs and instead spent a lot of time in front of the bars of other pubs around the town.

With a designated cellar man working in the pub for very long shifts six days a week, Andy's two main tasks seemed to be opening the door for the cleaners in the morning and locking it again when the pub was closed for the night. Admittedly, there was up to sixteen hours between these two jobs but managers like Andy never seemed to do that much in between with most tasks delegated to his cellar man. Most of Andy's time in between opening and closing was spent watching TV upstairs or in the town's other Tetley pubs. His sobriety was sporadic especially at the weekend and often when he arrived back into the pub to show his face for the last hour or so he could be disagreeable and arrogant and sometimes with an occasional downright nasty streak. His ability to turn any calm situation into a hostile one was quite spectacular given his total belief in his own view. It was his pub and he had to be top dog.

At the end of this particular Friday night as Phil was enjoying a pint and contemplating a return to loafing, the poker suggestion surprised the assembled crowd because they had never occurred before. Phil didn't really know how to play, and neither did the others, but they went along with it whilst they were finishing their drinks.

The game started and in the early hands, Andy kept losing and Phil kept winning. More hands were played and one or two people started to quit, but not Andy. He kept playing and continued to lose even more and it wasn't long before he was consistently losing game after game. None of the other players knew what they were doing. To them it was all just a bit of fun until they had lost a few quid at which stage they bailed out. Phil also knew nothing but he was the one that was cleaning up. Andy was doing all the talking about what to do and how to play but he wasn't winning a single hand. Phil's interest in the game was developing as the pile of cash in front of him kept getting bigger and he was in no rush to go home, especially as the beers kept coming. It got to the point where there was just Phil and Andy left. Phil offered to end the game, but Andy refused, insisting that he be given the chance to win his money back and so they settled in for a late-night head to head.

Whether it was down to Phil's successful bluffing, Andy's arrogance, his intoxication or a combination, Phil just kept winning more and more of Andy's money. Andy couldn't understand what was happening. He refused to be beaten and kept on demanding more chances to win his money back, yet every time he tried he just kept on losing more. Phil was even at the point where he was deliberately throwing hands and yet he kept on winning. Andy must have been a truly shocking poker player or maybe he was just too drunk to be able to compute what was going on. Phil even offered to give him his money back without playing, but Andy refused. It became compulsive viewing for those watching, seeing the normally cocksure Andy being done over by someone who had just walked into the pub that night. The money situation was getting more and more fraught and Andy's lovely wife, Mandy, was getting more and more upset, telling him to stop playing and pleading with him to not lose any more money. Mandy had a savings box that she had started when she became pregnant. In it she put the money she would have spent on cigarettes to be put aside for the baby. When it got to the point that the baby savings were going to be raided - despite Phil offering to give him his money back - Mandy's exasperated tears were enough to bring the game to an end and Andy finally quit, well into the early hours of the morning.

It wasn't quite the evening Phil had been expecting and he left for home with a pocketful of Andy's cash, grateful to make it out in one piece. He called back down the next day when I was back on duty and I had already heard about this memorable evening. He had wanted to avoid bumping into

Andy but he did want to collect his wages. He propped up the bar and had a nervous couple of pints whilst we chatted and waited for Andy to come back. When Andy arrived, Phil looked very apprehensive as Andy approached him. 'Phil!' was the warm greeting he gave him, quickly followed by 'What hours can you do for me this week?'

And so began the start of a great friendship, established through a love of Tetley drunk in often vast quantities. We were young, single and irresponsible and we both loved our Tetley. Phil knew plenty of pubs that I hadn't been to and we were to spend a lot of time working together and when we weren't in the pub serving beer, we would often be in a pub drinking it. It was to be a real golden age in our lives and working there over that Christmas and into the Spring of 1992 didn't feel like work at all because we were having so much fun and drinking so much beer.

My relationship with beer changed significantly and forever. I was to drink more of it, enjoy it more and visit a lot more pubs than I ever had. We quickly bonded over our appreciation of Tetley as we put the hard hours in at the Portman over Christmas and New Year. The late-night poker challenges were never repeated and, with the group bonding well and a good team in place and working well together, Andy was hanging around even less, confident that the pub was in safe hands. He began appearing in the bar later and later in the evening which suited us fine. And credit to him, the poker night was forgotten and there was no bad blood. It was all water under the bridge.

Phil loved his Tetley and knew where to get a good pint of it. He had been a convert for several years by this stage having had a two-year head start on me. He too had a short-lived flirt with the Allan Fold before discovering the pleasures of the Big Six. It didn't take long before we were soon drinking Tetley at the Portman, the Upper George and the Brass Cat in the town centre as well as spending far too much time in the Big Six. We would hunt out other Tetley pubs around the town and further afield because there was no shortage of Tetley houses in our corner of West Yorkshire.

Whilst all that was going on, a plan also came together in the space of a couple of days that sent me into Christmas 1991 in especially high spirits. One cold December morning I took an early morning train to London. After heading out to Sutton for an interview I headed back into London and then up to Sunderland for a night in a bed and breakfast before another interview the next day. The trip to Sutton saw me getting a job working in France for a camping holiday company that would start the following April and I was also offered an unconditional place at Sunderland Polytechnic after I returned from France. The place was offered as soon as I walked into what I was expecting to be a tough interview. I couldn't believe my luck or have been more pleased. Almost a year after making the decision to quit work and go to college, the plan had finally come together. I also had the bonus adventure of leaving home to go and work in France which was a country I had a real fondness for after camping holidays as a child.

In an impulsive moment, I quit my day job early in the New Year rather than waiting the extra couple of months before going to France. My heart was no longer in office work now that I knew I was leaving and, besides, Phil and I were too busy enjoying ourselves in and out of the Portman. Plus, April didn't seem that long to wait.

With the benefit of hindsight, January was not the best month to find yourself unemployed and with little money. The coldest, darkest and most miserable month of the year was also the quietest month in the pub trade with many customers understandably short of cash after Christmas and New Year. Extra shifts were not as numerous after the festive period but at least I wasn't going into the office every day. I still had my regular Portman shifts and the occasional extra and I felt enormously liberated after three years of work.

Whilst the Portman only served Tetley bitter there were three lagers on the bar. It was a common brewery-owned pub offering of a standard main brand plus a cheaper brand and a premium one. In Tetley pubs at the time, the standard brand was the Australian 1980s marketing success story, Castlemaine XXXX. Websters pubs sold Fosters, the other equally successful Australian invasion which I believe was brewed at the Websters brewery in Halifax for a time. Lowenbrau Blue was the quite respectable premium offering that hardly anybody bought and the cheaper was Skol, popular amongst price conscious customers (around £1.20 per pint compared to around £1.50 for Castlemaine).

Skol was forgettable as a beer, but there were some memorable adverts for it at the time especially with the cartoon character Hagar the Horrible. I always chuckled at the one with a bar full of Vikings drinking and thrusting their glasses in the air chanting 'Skol, Skol, Skol, Skol...' There's one gormless looking Viking slumped at the bar and not joining in and he is asked 'Why aren't you singing our drinking song?' 'Erm, I've forgotten the words' was the reply. Hilarious, and on YouTube.

I was surprised to discover courtesy of Wikipedia, so it must be true, that Skol was created through a collaboration of Allied Breweries, the owner of Tetley, Labatts of Canada, Pripps-Bryggerierna of Sweden and Unibra of Belgium in 1964. They had a plan to create a global beer brand to be licensed and manufactured worldwide. Apparently, and again according to lazy research on Wikipedia, it is currently the most popular beer in Brazil, having overtaken the much more palatable Brazilian beer Brahma. I have been to Brazil and I don't ever remember seeing Skol in any of the bars we went to. Having said that, I don't remember much of my time in the bars of Brazil and after getting robbed at knife-point my memory of Brazil has been somewhat tainted. Although a successful brand may have been created, especially in terms of longevity and apparent success in Brazil, it wasn't the 'horribly good lager' that the adverts claimed.

The standard lager brand, Castlemaine XXXX, was a brand for those of us that came of age in the 1980s. It wasn't that bad to drink compared to Fosters which always seems to have an unpleasant aftertaste and both beers had some great advertising. We'd been sold all things Australian in the second half of the 1980s from *Neighbours* to *Crocodile Dundee* via *Prisoner: Cell Block H* and the *Paul Hogan Show* for those of us that stayed watching late night TV at the weekend when we were too young to be going out.

As well as TV and movies, those of us growing up in rugby league country also had our own mid-1980s Australian invasion. Although there had been occasional overseas players in the game since the 1970s, at the beginning of the 1984-85 season, the domestic game became dominated by big and small name Australian players after rule changes governing the number of overseas players were removed in 1984. Many clubs signed Australian players, with the bigger clubs like Hull and Wigan grabbing some of the big-name stars. The immediate impact in Halifax was that the club was flooded with cheaper and less high profile Australian imports that displaced players that had served the club loyally for the previous few years, but who could never keep the club in the old First Division. The club was regularly promoted and relegated through the early 1980s and had been promoted at the end of the previous season. Many of the players that achieved promotion were finding themselves pushed aside by new arrivals.

The huge shock was the sacking of the coach, Colin Dixon. Dixon, who died tragically early in 1993, was a legend of the club from the 1960s which was the club's last era of success and he was the world's most expensive player when he was sold by Halifax to Salford for £15 000 in 1968. He was replaced by a relatively unknown Australian called Chris Anderson who was coming to the end of his playing career and had found himself at Hull Kingston Rovers. A glittering career in coaching was ahead of him, including coaching the Australian national team, and it began in Halifax where in his first season, 1984-85, he steered the team away from relegation. Astonishingly, the following season the club won the First Division Championship and the season after that, 1986-87, the team won the Challenge Cup at Wembley. He returned to Australia after taking Halifax to the final at Wembley the following year but they were well beaten by Wigan in the final.

Australian lager was all the rage at the time, along with Scott and Sharlene, and there was some great TV advertising by both big brands as they fought for market share. Fosters and Castlemaine dominated choice in the town through the sheer number of Websters and Tetley pubs. Although Fosters continues its foul-tasting presence, it's strange to think that a beer that was at one time as prominent as Castlemaine could disappear, but disappear it did in 2009 when the Castlemaine licensing agreement was not renewed.

As Phil and I bonded over lots of Tetley that Winter, work at the Portman began to get increasingly silly. New 'rules,' introduced by Phil, began to be adopted. The most basic was that always on Friday and Saturday nights there had to be a half pint of Tetley sitting on the back counter. These halves of Tetley were merely the sipping drinks, though they were rarely sipped and generally went in a couple of mouthfuls. A rule was introduced to supplement these sipping drinks when at regular intervals during the night, a call was made and we were to stop whatever it was we were doing, even if the pub was full and we were busy serving, and we were to pull a half pint and down it in one. After a wince and a belch, it was straight back into serving the throngs as if nothing had happened. Of course, this far from subtle behaviour could only happen when Andy wasn't around and, thankfully, he rarely was.

We always managed to get away with it. Customers didn't even seem to mind and quite often encouraged us. It only took a few seconds away from serving time to quickly pull another half of Tetley whilst other poured pints were settling. Although it originated as a daft game, another reason that encouraged us to do it was the generosity of the customers. On most weekend evenings, you would have at least half a dozen drinks bought for you and usually far more, plus any that had been 'banked' from during the weekday shifts that hadn't been taken. Beer was relatively cheap at the time and the regulars were very generous.

As well as the generosity of customers, another factor that helped with this drinking was that we drank hand pulled cask ale. As everyone knows, beer is only served properly in the north, that is with the decent creamy head from pulling the beer through the sparkler. Being in Yorkshire, some drinkers only wanted a tiny slither of head on their beer so that they could get maximum value for money from their pint. However, most drinkers wanted anything up to a centimetre of head on their pint so that the pint kept a creamy consistency with every mouthful and the head lasted for the duration of the pint, clinging to the side of the glass as the pint was drunk. With pint sized glasses all these centimetres of head were accumulated because for every pint of beer being sold, not quite a full pint of beer was being served and they soon added up, especially, in a high-volume beer pub like the Portman. A lot of 'surplus' beer was accumulated and a reasonable amount of it went down our necks. It was very wrong, of course it was, to just help ourselves as we did without keeping an accurate tally of whether we were drinking beers that had been bought for us or not. To all intents and purposes, it was theft. We got away with it because of the volume of the beer sold, the substantial number of drinks we had bought and by pouring all pints with a decent head which customers could then asked to be topped up if necessary. At the weekend, the pub was so busy that even people particularly choosy about the size of the head would let a millimetre or two go to get away from the bar and enjoy their night out. The more head that was in the glasses, the more beer there was in the barrel down in the cellar. Tetley stock-takes were always in a substantial surplus, regardless of our halves.

At work, we began enjoying ourselves more and more and the levels of work-related drunkenness increased rapidly. Phil was the chief instigator and in me he found someone more than willing to join in. Plus, like him, I could hold a lot of ale and still function.

As well as plenty of drinking when we were working, there was the dilemma of what to do on our breaks. When doing the double shift on Saturdays we got a thirty-minute break in the late afternoon. Rather than resting and maybe getting something to eat, we walked briskly to the nearby Westgate pub where we would drink a couple of pints of their excellent Tetley before heading back.

But we couldn't leave it there. Instead of being sensible, we got stupidly competitive about how many pints we could drink before returning to the Portman. We only had half an hour, but before long we were drinking four pints of Tetley in that time. The walk back to the Portman was a slower and we were considerably more unsteady on our feet. Arriving back behind the bar a bit light headed and woozy, we were then all set for whatever a Saturday night could throw at us.

Even for two big blokes who were capable of holding their beer, four pints in half an hour is going to leave even the most capable of drinkers a little sluggish whilst the body processed the rapid booze onslaught. To deal with this, Patrick dreamed up a little 'pick-me-up' to get us back into the swing of things and a barrel change was always a good excuse for one. When a barrel of lager was changed, a small amount had to be pulled through the pipes before the fresh clear lager from the new barrel was flowing. This 'pull-through' lager was frothy and cloudy and it was thrown down the sink for a reason. Cellar equipment has improved removing the need to pull-through, but Phil didn't like to see it go to waste. Instead, when a barrel was changed he would pour the pull-through into a jug rather than the conventional steel bucket. He'd then let it settle before pouring it into half pint glasses. The glasses weren't filled up though. To counter any bad taste from the lager, enough space was left to top the glasses up with some cider, making them half pint snakebites. We downed them in one and then had a good glug of Tetley to take the taste away. They didn't taste great, but they did pick us up.

Looking back, it seems inconceivable that we got through the evening. We were in high spirits thanks to all the beer and no-one really seemed to notice. We were doing our job and doing it well but it was always a relief to down tools at 11pm when time was called and we could sit down and have a breather.

The pub was invariably in a mess by closing time on weekend evenings, but we would all get stuck in to clean up and when it was finished, the conversation turned to 'Where next?' The late options in Halifax hadn't improved much since Crossleys' Bar had closed a few years earlier, but there was still a choice which ranged from terrible to dire. We went for dire because if we went for dire, we got in for free. The Tram Shed and the Zoo Bar were in a building at the top of the town centre that once housed Mr Dobb's Pizza Factory, an early modern restaurant in the town which was very popular in the early 1980s. It was possibly the first pizza restaurant in the town centre. If it wasn't the first, it was certainly the first one that I went to. It was a very special family treat in the school holidays when we sometimes went for 'tea' after a day trip. When it closed, around 1988, it housed various grim nightclubs and much later the very pleasant Hairy Lemon, though sadly that has also since closed.

It would be at least midnight by the time we got there and there was a minor celebrity feeling when we turned up en masse, invariably worse for wear, and the guys on the door welcomed us as 'the boys from the Portman.' A lot of the staff and customers were also Portman regulars at the weekend.

Once we were inside we headed straight to the bar where, not surprisingly, there was no decent beer available and so we would have a few bottles of headache-inducing Newcastle Brown Ale. It certainly was an advantage having a lot of beer before going because it really was an awful place. It was a dark, dingy, run down rock club and on Saturday nights it was full of mainly male heavy metal fans in what seemed to be a standard uniform of big hair, spandex and denim jackets with the sleeves rolled up. They would be in groups on the dancefloor playing air guitar and headbanging and those not on the dancefloor tended to hang around in groups doing the same thing. It was hardly surprising that there weren't many women in there. If we were lucky, they played the then omnipresent *Smells Like Teen Spirit* by Nirvana and maybe *Sweet Child of Mine* by Guns 'n' Roses, that one in particular getting the head-banging air-guitarists really going. The rest of the music was an awful metal dirge which we could handle for no more than an hour and a couple of bottles of brown ale. We would then stumble out in the early hours to the famous pie and peas caravan that was just down the road for a late-night snack.

February became March and the weekend shifts became even more rowdy. The pull through snakebites moved onto pouring ourselves non-pull through snakebites as pick-me-ups with a half of Tetley to wash it down with and to take the taste out of our mouths. Somehow, we remained competent behind the bar, or at least we thought we were, and with the place being so busy, nobody really seemed to notice just how pissed we were. We would never have got away with it in a quiet pub. The trick we learned early was to make sure that if we were pissed, to make sure that we weren't as pissed as Andy. It was a rule that worked well and that we followed for months until Phil's judgement got the better of him.

Towards the end of our time there and at the end of one Saturday night we were especially leathered. After ringing the bell for time, I poured two pints of Tetley at 11pm for our quick break, one for me and one for Phil. We were due a free half at closing time anyway and I was feeling some rare guilt given the amount we had drunk over the previous eight hours. I rang the two additional halves through the till which was £1.22. All was well until Phil, in a drunkenly foolish and completely unnecessary move, voided the transaction off the till. It was stupid. There was absolutely no reason for him to do it and he wasn't even paying for the beers. What the fool hadn't realised was that Andy was sat on a stool at the end of the bar watching the whole thing. As we turned towards the exit he asked us 'Have you lads just bought some beer? You've got two pints and there is nothing showing on the till.' We hadn't even realized that he had returned to the pub from wherever he had been. He just stared at us with a glazed expression on his face waiting for an answer.

We were addled on the beer and the snakebites and the normally confident Phil realised he had overstepped the mark. I couldn't think and was gripped in panic. We came out from behind the bar and out of sight of Andy in the passageway from the bar to the pub we both looked at each and simultaneously said 'FUCK!!' We knew we were on the weakest of weak grounds. We had been rumbled and didn't have a response, at least immediately anyway. It was a stupid thing to get into a whole load of trouble over. Thankfully, after what seemed an age, Phil stepped up to the mark. I had been floundering. I couldn't think straight and was in a panic about how to deal with the situation. Phil then very confidently said that the two halves were drinks that had been bought for him earlier in the evening that he hadn't been able to take and he had forgotten to tell me. I breathed a huge sigh of relief and waited for Andy's response. He didn't look convinced but he at least gave the impression of believing us and didn't dwell on it so maybe, after all, he was more pissed than us. We survived to fight another day.

April came quickly and it was time to move on. It had been so much fun over the previous eight months and especially the last four which had turned into one long party. My start date was finally confirmed for mid-April and, by a remarkable coincidence, Phil's departure date for a job he had got overseas was the same day, both of us needing to be in London on the same Sunday morning. We could finish at the Portman at the same time and head to London together.

It would have been rude if we didn't have a bit of a leaving do. We began at the canal-side Moorings pub in Sowerby Bridge where we made a rare change from ale and drank some bottled Lion beers from South Africa. It was warm enough to go outside and overlooking the canal on a balmy Spring evening we were calm and reflective as we mulled over the bizarre last few months we had enjoyed and contemplated what might await us overseas. We then jumped into a cab and went to the Portman where all hell broke loose.

Phil ordered us snakebites, something we had never ordered before. In fact, we would refuse to serve them if someone asked for them when we were working. Although they were surprised and rather bemused with the request, the staff poured them for us. After we sat down, Phil bizarrely produced a small bottle of pre-prepared vodka and blue curacao of all things which he topped the snakebite up with. We never did spirits and so this was a first. It turned our pints into sickly tasting, turquoise coloured drinks he called green diesels. It wasn't particularly subtle given the distinct colour of our pints and it was the kind of behaviour we would have chucked people out for. But on a quiet Thursday early evening and in the spirit of one rule for one and one rule for another, we drank them, collected our outstanding wages and said our thanks and goodbyes to Andy (I wanted to keep him on side for work during the holidays). We headed off to the Upper George where the sickliness of the green diesels was washed away with plenty of their great Tetley which would be our last decent pints for more than six months.

After some bad dancing and watching the inevitable fight in the Cats' Bar, our last night in the town centre wouldn't have been complete without a final pie and peas from the caravan at the top of George's Square. This caravan was a legendary weekend fixture for years before the town centre was completely overrun with take-aways. From there you got a hot pork pie, chips, mushy peas and mint sauce for £1.50. It was terrific value and they always tasted delicious after a load of beer, although I never ate one sober to compare. The elderly Eastern European couple dished them out every Thursday, Friday and Saturday night without fail for years in all weathers. It was a popular place and there was always a queue. I hope they're enjoying a well-earned retirement after battling the elements and Halifax's drunks for so long with good grace and cracking grub. After the obligatory spillage of mushy peas down the shirt it was a stumble home to sleep off the green diesels. The Portman days had ended. I was leaving home and going to France.

7 HALIFAX PUBS

France was a blast and after returning from France in September, it was a quick turnaround before heading north to begin student life in Sunderland. The polytechnic I had gone to for the interview the previous December had now transformed into a university in the higher education shake up of that year. As well as gaining a university, Sunderland had also gained city status that year and their football team had reached the 1992 FA Cup final from the old second division in that final season before the arrival of the Premier League (they lost 2-0).

These positives amounted to little given the combination of the early 1990s recession and the painful transition the town was going through with the decline of its traditional industries along the River Wear and the imminent closure of the remaining colliery. The new and enlarged university did at least bring extra students into the town to spend their money on beer and Pot Noodles and it was amongst these throngs of Doc Martin wearing students that I wandered aimlessly around the town trying to find out where I was supposed to be going.

Sunderland was still home to the sizeable Vaux brewery and they still used horse-drawn drays to deliver beer around the town. They regularly passed my window overlooking Chester Road just outside the town centre and over at the brewery a slight change in the wind direction ensured the whole town knew there was a brew on. The Brewery Tap on the brewery site was a terrific old world pub reminding me very much of the Big Six, but despite some determined research it was difficult to find decent pubs in the town. With just one or two exceptions, neon, loud music and casual violence typified many of the pubs that we explored and none were particularly welcoming to students. It was a tough working-class town and gentrification and regeneration were still years away. Those that had jobs and some money coming in didn't seem bothered about character, tradition or decent beer when they could go to a pub and get served by a woman wearing a skimpy swimming costume and high heels whilst very loud dance music blasted away in the background. The huge increase in student numbers that year aggravated the town and gown divide and students tended to stick to the relative safety of the Students' Union bars or the student nights in the local nightclubs. There was at least one every night of the week and you had to have an NUS card or be a guest of someone with one to get in. The Students' Union wasn't great but it did sell kegged beer for 78p per pint. That seemed cheap but it wasn't the cheapest in the town. That honour went to the nightclub whose name is consigned to history that sold beer at their Tuesday night student night for 10p per pint. It didn't taste great, goodness knows where it came from and plenty of toilet time was needed the following day.

After a year in the north east I changed institutions and headed south to start at Reading University. Sunderland didn't live up to my expectations and it was to be at Reading that my real student experience would begin. It was a lot further away and trips home were few and far between because travelling was both expensive and a hassle. Getting to and from Sunderland was straightforward and didn't take too long but coming back from Reading seemed to take all day. It involved either a trip down the Thames Valley into Paddington, across London to Kings Cross and up the east coast line to Leeds for a local train back to Halifax, or the cheaper but much longer way was to take the cross-country train via Oxford, Birmingham and Sheffield to Leeds before catching the local to Halifax. Both routes were long, expensive and only done a few times a year.

Much as I loved living away and being a student, it was always nice to come home. After a long journey and months of southern beer that in Reading was tasteless Courage served flat with no sparkler, one of the few things that I missed was a good pint of northern ale.

On these rare journeys home a tradition began that was to last for over ten years. After getting off the train, I would walk up from Halifax railway station and go for a pint before getting the bus home. The first decent pub on the way to the bus stop was the then relatively new Tap and Spile at the end of Clare Road. It was an odd-looking pub that, as the Royal Oak, had been rebuilt in a deliberately mock Tudor style in the 1930s to replace an historic former coaching inn that at one time still had an eighteenth-century milestone giving the distance to London outside. It had a bit of a reputation, so we were led to believe, as the Royal Oak. Phil and I went in there once the previous year when we had decided to explore some of the town centre pubs that neither of us had visited before. It was in the dying days of its former life as the Royal Oak before its Tap and Spile refurbishment and it was alright. It was nothing special, just a big, open bland pub with no customers and average but certainly not dreadful beer.

We drank our pints, happy to have ticked it off the list of places we'd never been to and left the empty glasses on the bar as we generally did on the way out. We got a few metres down the road when we heard the door behind us and the sound of someone coming after us. We turned around and it was the landlord who was on the street smiling and waving as he said, 'Thanks a lot lads!' which was an admirable effort to go to.

By the end of 1993 when I returned from Reading for the first time, it had been refurbished and had become a Tap and Spile, a relatively short-lived chain with a focus on real ale from independent and smaller breweries in what was then still a brewery dominated town. It was given a nice make-over with lots of exposed floorboards and light pine pews and tables along with a good range of real ales. The quality of the beer was always exceptional and remained so for years before its decline with the collapse of the Tap and Spile chain in the 2000s. A subsequent re-opening as the Royal Oak was unsuccessful before another closure and yet another re-opening in the last couple of years as Dirty Dicks Real Ale Emporium. The name was dreadful but the focus on good beer was maintained. The owners moved on in 2017 and the name has reverted to the Royal Oak.

The pub's volatile future was still to come and in my early student days it was my new second favourite pub, after the Big Six of course. It was a very welcome sight after setting foot back in Yorkshire after a long train journey. The beer was always good and the first one would barely touch the sides as it slid down the throat followed by a couple of slightly slower, but still brisk, pints before heading up to the bus stop.

On one of these trips home I took a diversion to get the bus from a different stop and I passed a now long-gone arts supplies shop that also stocked prints from local artists. In the window was a large print in a style which I've since seen replicated elsewhere but it was a first for me at the time. It was an interpretation of the London Underground map but with the pubs of Halifax organised geographically (kind of) and by 'line.' Always short of Christmas gift ideas, I dropped a hint and Father Christmas brought me one.

More than twenty years later, I still have that print. It's a little battered after several house moves but I always like glancing at it and pondering how much things have changed and how many of the pubs on it have gone. The print was published in 1995 and it features a hundred and twenty pubs stretching from the town centre to Illingworth on the moorland north of town, westwards up the hill to King Cross and then down into Sowerby Bridge as well as areas south of the town centre like Siddal and Skircoat Green. It chose the substantial natural barrier of Beacon Hill to the east to exclude the nearby settlements of Southowram, Northowram and Hipperholme. By 2013 when this project was first being considered, sixty eight of the hundred and twenty on the map remained open, a decline of over forty per cent in less than twenty years. The numbers have changed constantly. More have closed and some that were closed have re-opened. Some brand-new pubs have opened, including two Wetherspoon's, but nothing like the number that have closed. There are a lot fewer pubs around the town than there were in the mid-1990s.

Looking at the map, it is quite depressing to see the names of so many places that we used to go to that have long gone. Amongst all the doom and gloom there are signs of rejuvenation and reinvention and perhaps the best example is in Sowerby Bridge, at the western end of the map. It has bucked the trend and has seen a renaissance not only in pubs, but in restaurants, apartments and general desirability. It is in a narrow valley bottom where the Calder and Ryburn Valleys meet and mills and factories jostled for space between the road, railway, canal and river. Terraced housing stretched up the steep hillsides from the valley floor and open fields and farmhouses were just a stone's throw away making it an industrial hub surrounded by greenery.

Most of the industry has gone with many mills either demolished or converted to apartments but its transport links have served it well. The canal was a focal point for the town's regeneration especially after the blockage at Tuel Lane was reopened in the mid-1990s. Instead of having two canal termini in the town, the Rochdale Canal and the Calder and Hebble Navigation were reconnected for the first time in many years after road alterations had severed the waterway allowing narrowboats to travel again across the Pennines between Manchester and Wakefield. The railway station allowed it to be a commutable and affordable base for those working in Bradford, Leeds and Manchester. Creative types priced out of nearby Hebden Bridge settled there and wealthy professionals snapped up nearby farm houses for relative peanuts. The town looks a lot smarter than it did and a smattering of new pubs and restaurants have opened, including a thriving vegan restaurant which would have been unheard of in the 'old' Sowerby Bridge.

More people than ever head down there to visit the pubs, but despite the success of places like the Jubilee Refreshment Rooms on the once uninviting Sowerby Bridge station, the terrific Hog's Head brewpub and The Works, just off the main street housed in a converted workshop (at least until it unexpectedly closed in November 2016), as well as some other new and reopened ventures, 40% of the pubs that were open at the time of the print in 1995 have gone. The Stirk Bridge, the Royal Hotel, the Town Hall Tavern, the Engineers, the Rams Head, Bridges and the Brothers Grimm have gone as has, more recently, the Puzzle Hall Inn. The Commercial did close but was re-built and re-opened as a Wetherspoon's and the Bull's Head was closed for several years before being renovated and re-opened.

Several new places have opened over the last ten years and the town's pubs seem to be doing well. It draws people to what are on the whole nice pubs and being on one street, it is easy to find somewhere else if you want a change or a pub crawl. Except for the Stirk Bridge which used to be a nice Tetley pub tucked out of the way of the main drag and the Puzzle Hall which always seemed to be popular, a common theme amongst the closed pubs was that they were awful, or at least they had become awful by the time they finally closed their doors. Many of them were tough pubs from the old Sowerby Bridge, and there's nothing wrong with that. But, they had become neglected and scruffy with poor drinks offerings and bad atmospheres. Times had changed, but they hadn't. There were a lot more people coming into the town and spending money, but they weren't spending it in grotty unloved pubs when there were much better alternatives.

There had always been a small but lively community based around the canal even in the days when the canal was severed. There is a busy former wharf area with narrowboat dwellers and some popular canal-side pubs. One was the Navigation, its name itself alluding to the adjacent Calder and Hebble Navigation. It was run for years by the badly permed and wonderfully eccentric Dave and the pub was known for its perfect Tetley bitter, convivial atmosphere and great home-cooked food made by Dave. An anecdote I heard in a pub once was that apparently one of his creations was the Dave o' Grady Dinner which was served in a traditional heavy ceramic dog bowl. This he humorously called DoG's Dinner.

Bob and I spent time in there in our early days of venturing out to pubs after he had a short spell working there. Dave could be charming, funny and unpredictable all within the space of five minutes. There was rarely a dull moment when he was around though. When he left the pub, he took his flair for food and love of the canal into a very successful narrowboat cruise and dine business before finally retiring. The pub also got exposure in the late 1980s and early 1990s when it was used for some scenes in the Dennis Waterman and Sue Francis series *Stay Lucky* which saw a lot of filming around the canal and the town. More recently the area was used for a lot of scenes in *Happy Valley*.

Also linked with the canal was what became a Sowerby Bridge institution and an early mover in spearheading change in the town. The Moorings was converted from former warehouses in the former canal wharf. It offered picturesque views overlooking narrowboats in the basin and it served good beer. What made the Moorings different was its bottled beer menu, and especially the Belgian beers. In the early 1990s in Halifax at least, this was something very different. Pubs were owned by the breweries and the bottled beer choice was usually very limited and very boring, beers like Holsten Pils and Budweiser being standard. The Portman used to stock

Molson Dry and Lowenbrau in bottles and I think the same bottles were on the shelf when I left that were there when I started. They just didn't sell (unlike the bottles of Diamond White and 'K' cider). The Moorings was different and it stocked a wide range of bottled beers from around the world and provided matching glasses to drink them out of. There was even a menu and tasting notes on the tables, years before hipsters started doing it.

Less salubrious than the Moorings but safer than some of Sowerby Bridge's fighting pubs was the curiously named Puzzle Hall Inn. Originally a small brew-house with a tower on the small almost cottage like building, the tiny pub had a fiercely loyal crowd who would easily fill its two small rooms. The bar was so small it made the one at the Big Six look palatial. There was barely room for one person to work behind it, never mind the two or three that were needed at the weekend. It was popular with the artistic and musical crowd and it was also unusual because it was a Wards pub. Wards was a smallish Sheffield brewery that had been taken over in the early 1970s by Vaux of Sunderland, a brewery that also had one or two isolated outposts in the area. When greedy financiers, rather than a lack of customers, closed Vaux in 1999, Wards went with it. The Puzzle survived and seemed to thrive until suddenly closing in 2016.

Heading through Sowerby Bridge westwards takes you through a couple of increasingly picturesque and semi-rural settlements before the road climbs and winds onto the moors and the Pennine hills. Heading east and back towards Halifax is very different though. To begin with there is Bolton Brow, a very steep hill which at one time was crowded with pubs in its lower stages. Now, only the Shepherds' Rest remains. For years, it was best avoided as one of Sowerby Bridge's notorious fighting pubs but in the early 2000s it was acquired and sympathetically renovated by the Ossett Brewery who were expanding their pub estate. It continues its business quietly and unassumingly selling the excellent Ossett beers as well as a good range of guest ales.

The last stop just before reaching the summit at King Cross was once The Wellington which was a small Tetley local for years before it fell on tough times. It was taken over by a trio of locals through a questionable and since defunct pub leasing company and enjoyed a terrific renaissance in the mid-2000s under its new name of The George. It quickly and deservedly got into CAMRA's Good Beer Guide on the strength of its quality beers and it became a popular real ale destination until a fall out between the investors, a change of ownership and the collapse of the owning company sent it into decline and a cycle of closures and failed re-openings as well as changing its name back to the Wellington. Its misfortune was complete in 2015 when it was badly damaged by a fire started by the landlord in which one man tragically died.

After the steep climb up from the Calder Valley, King Cross lies on the brow of the hill before a more gradual descent down into the town of Halifax. King Cross has fared better than some areas with most of the pubs open in 1995 still open now. There have been just two casualties, the West End and the Trafalgar. Of those that are open, the William IV had a great reputation for many years and was known for the quality of its Tetley bitter and it still soldiers on without the beer that gave it its reputation.

To the left of the main road down into the town centre from King Cross lies the huge Victorian urban and industrial spread of the town as it expanded and moved further westwards thanks to geographical restrictions in all other directions. This was, and remains, a densely-populated area with terraced housing of varying sizes from back to backs to substantial villas and even one or two grand mansions, all within a relatively confined space. Whilst there was substantial demolition of housing around the town centre for slum clearance and road improvement schemes, much of the housing stock clustered around Gibbet Street, Hanson Lane, Parkinson Lane, Lister Lane and Hopwood Lane remained and began to be populated by the arriving Pakistani community from the 1960s. Much of the industry has disappeared but there were still numerous pubs back in 1995. With just a couple of exceptions on the peripheries, all the Victorian pubs have gone. The Golden Lion as well as The Cherry Tree, The Buccaneer, The Duke of Edinburgh, The Tavern, The Granby, The Nook, The Clarence and The Woodcock are no more.

To the north of the town the areas of Ovenden and Illingworth have also fared badly. These were once small isolated almost rural communities and in the case of Illingworth it was just a cluster of farmhouses on wild open moorland until massive house-building of both council and private housing before and after the war. The pubs that served them have almost all gone. One of the largest and grandest, the Ovenden Way, a huge 1930s roadhouse style pub built along with the council housing between the wars was another pub that recently suffered a major fire.

To have fared even worse is the area of Boothtown, a working-class area stretching up yet another long steep hill, this time in the direction of Queensbury and on to Bradford. Sitting above the former Crossleys' Carpets mills of Dean Clough, the area is known for the workers' 'model' village of Akroyden built by Victorian benefactor and mill owner William Ackroyd in 1859 and used in the filming of Alan Bennett's play *A Grand Day Out* in the early 1970s. It would have been quite a pub crawl in 1995 with the trek up the hill guaranteed to generate a thirst, several pit stops at convenient distances to stop for a pint with the reward of some fabulous views from the top. Although you can still have a pint in the Flying Dutchman (if you really wanted to) at the bottom of the hill, The Coach and Horses, the Friendly, Foggys, the New Inn, the New Delight and the

Red Lion have gone, all in the space of less than a mile. The Sportsman, set back from the main road is still open, though its small dry ski slope which created a lot of excitement when it opened in the 1980s is looking a bit worse for wear.

A little further out of the town heading south is the former Chartist hotspot turned affluent middle-class area of Skircoat Green which has lost nearly half of its pubs since 1995. I wasn't sad to see the end of the Commercial even though it had good Tetley. The landlord was amongst the most consistently rude and unfriendly I have encountered over the years. The Murgatroyd had some difficulties but now seems to have re-established itself as one of two locals' pubs on Skircoat Green, but I was sad to see its traditional tap room and lounge layout removed to create one open room when I went in recently. The other remaining pub is the Standard of Freedom that we met earlier.

The decline of the nearby (to home) Stafford Arms surprised me the most. For years, this was a very popular pub with a decent crowd in every night and very busy at weekends. It used to be a Whitbread pub and their Trophy Bitter was just about the only other beer I drank apart from Tetley in the late 1980s. Something went badly wrong in the early 2000s and its decline was fast and irreversible. It was constantly struggling with a revolving door of tenants for a few years. One story doing the rounds at the time was that someone thought he had bought the pub when he had in fact only bought a lease and was not expecting to be paying rent on top of that. When things went wrong he allegedly stripped the place down to taking skirting boards and plug sockets off the wall and pouring concrete down the drains to spite whoever had done the deal with him. It went on the market as a freehold sale for almost silly money given the size and the potential and has since been converted into a curry restaurant.

Surprisingly, given the general decline of the town centre over the years, the rate of pub closures has not been as severe as I would have expected. Of the thirty-eight pubs open and on the map in 1995, at the time of writing twenty-six, or 75%, remain trading. Added to that are some new openings including two Wetherspoon's as well as smaller venues like the Circle Lounge, the impressive Victorian Craft Beer Café which is an excellent pub with an impressive range of beers. There are also three newly opened and very nice micro-pubs.

Whilst a lot have somehow managed to stay open and some names have changed, many of them are nothing like they used to be. All the old pubs are much quieter, even at the weekend, and sadly so many of them seem to be in a race to the bottom with heavily discounted Carling, Fosters and John Smiths Smooth and often opening from as early in the morning. There are some awful, unappealing pubs in the town but thankfully amongst all the gloom some gems have remained unscathed and have even prospered in a declining market.

Some old favourites have kept going, doing what they do well and focusing on the beer. Just outside the town centre is the award-winning Three Pigeons with its art-Deco multi-roomed interior giving it heritage status. There is also the Ring o' Bells, an ancient pub just across from the Minster in one of the oldest parts of the town and the Royal Oak, where we began.

Thankfully, being that little bit further out of the town centre they don't attract the Saturday night crowd that sadly blights so much of the town centre. They have their own regular customers, drawn to them for the quality of the beer and being able to drink it in a nice pub. There are still some nice places to go but the days of hordes of people drifting round the different pub circuits are long gone and won't be coming back. People are voting with their feet and their wallets and going elsewhere, to Huddersfield, Leeds and Manchester or to much nicer pubs, bars and restaurants just outside the town in places like Dean Clough where there is less potential for aggravation and less vomit on the pavements. The fights at the taxi rank are much reduced because there always seems to be an available taxi rather than the wait-induced scrapping of years earlier.

The friendly little cluster of the Tetley pubs and their crowd of regulars has also long gone. The buildings might remain but they are nothing compared to what they were. The Portman and Pickles name went in 2012 when it was renamed the Jubilee. The last time I walked past it was proudly displaying details of its happy hour which started at 9am. The last time I went in was very briefly on a Saturday night a few years ago and there was one barmaid and four customers, one of whom had badly inked prison tattoos across his forehead. When I worked there we had five people just behind the bar. It typified the decline and neglect that was typical of so many pubs that had thrived as brewery-owned tied houses and quickly disintegrated under changed ownership. No-one loved that pub any more. It was a mess. Pictures had been prised off the walls, wallpaper was ripped and upholstery was torn. It was an awful, depressing experience especially after knowing what it was like in its good times.

At the time of the map in 1995, the town centre was still very popular. Breweries still owned pubs and the Websters brewery was still a year away from closure. As well as a vibrant pub scene in the town centre, some out of town pubs were also doing well. As well as bustling community locals like the Stafford Arms, always busy on a weekend evening, some pubs out on the hills did a roaring trade in the late 1980s and early 1990s. Some of these were a considerable drive or taxi journey and included places like The Fleece in Greetland (closed), The Fleece in Ripponden (closed and re-opened) and the very popular and even harder to get to Blue Ball in Norland (closed) with its huge car park giving an idea just how popular it was at one time.

It is sad to see the decline in the town centre. It used to be such a bustling place and it was a great night out where you would always bump into people you knew. The biggest employer, the head office of the Halifax Building Society, gave the smarter pubs plenty of trade, especially on a Friday night with many going straight from the office to the pub in places like Maggie's or Maine Street, but that changed with the financial crash in 2008 and the fall-out from the subsequent take-over by Lloyds. Maggie's finally closed and the building is up for sale.

Above Maggie's, in the days of big independent investment in the pubs of the town, was Ma Bakers, created from scratch in 1988 with a lot of thought and expense and done with a 1930s Chicago theme. It was opened by the Turczaks who were an entrepreneurial local family who from humble origins in a King Cross greasy spoon went on to create more and more ambitious pub and restaurant ventures. Their formula seemed to be to start a business and do it well, not on the cheap, and then build it up, make it successful then sell it on and watch it disintegrate. Ma Bakers went from a stylish pub with ornate wooden bars and walls lined with memorabilia to a filthy, stripped dump, badly painted in black and purple before it finally closed. It was such a waste because it was such a different place to go and it was very impressive when it opened.

Another one of their ventures was the Hughes Corporation at the bottom of town that brought American-themed dining to the town years before TGI Fridays arrived. Again, it became successful, was sold on and has now been empty for years with a wooden sign rotting and just waiting to collapse onto some unsuspecting pedestrian.

The Brass Cat and the Portman and Pickles were good pubs, very different, but each had their own charm and they both had consistently good Tetley beer. Across the courtyard from the Brass Cat was the Upper George, an historic pub in the town that dated from the early 18th century although the current building dates from the 1820s. Because it was favoured by bikers and heavy metal fans, it had a completely unjust reputation as the roughest pub in town where gangs of bikers would give you a kicking just for daring to walk through the door. In fact, in the early 1990s the Upper George was probably one of the safest and best run pubs in the town centre. It was always packed and had a fabulous rock-oriented jukebox playing some great music and keeping a close eye on the pub was the eagle-eyed landlord Ian.

Unlike some of the absent Tetley landlords around the town, at the weekend when the pub was especially busy, Ian was there, keeping an eye on things. He was rarely behind the bar, but he was there standing inside the door and overlooking everything. He had an intimidating presence but he was very friendly and approachable. That said, he was a big lad and he took no nonsense. He wasn't looking for trouble and he wanted everyone to have a good time, but if there was trouble then he would deal with it, although his very presence was a deterrent. Any bad behaviour, drugs, rudeness to the staff and you were out. Rumour has it that he retired early to a farm in South Africa and when he left the takings subsequently fell through the floor. It didn't take long for the pub to get quieter and quieter and you could have the pick of seats in the back at the weekend, something that never used to be possible. Some say he was offered a blank cheque to come back. He turned it down.

Andy didn't fare quite so well. Not long after Phil and I left, there was a brewery stock check. The Tetley was in surplus which was amazing considering the amount that we drank, but they found a staggering amount of Castlemaine XXXX cans missing. Nobody ever drank Castlemaine cans apart from Andy. We deliberately avoided it because it was Andy's drink and we didn't want to be tainted if there were any problems. Well, the brewery had found a problem, and a big one. There were an awful lot of cans missing, some say hundreds. Whatever the number was, and whether it was an excuse to get rid of him, who knows, but stock was missing and he was shown the door. He was a bit of an arse but there was no pleasure in seeing him gone, especially with a young family to support. It was quite a cushy life as a Tetley manager at the time with a roof over his head and he would probably never get it so good again. I really hope he's doing OK but it's a face I've not seen or heard of for years.

His loss was everyone else's gain because he was replaced by a terrific bloke called Simon who was a pleasure to work for and he brought a much cheerier atmosphere to the pub. I made some guest appearances in the Christmas and Easter holidays in 1993 and early 1994 but those silly days with Phil were never repeated. There were no snakebite pick-me-ups or four pint breaks at the Westgate, but it was still a nice bustling place to work. As I got established at Reading the visits back were fewer and shorter in length and so I didn't even call ahead looking for hours. I stopped working there whilst it was still enjoying its good times and thankfully I wasn't around to see its sorry decline over the next few years.

The decline of Halifax's town centre pubs coincided with the rise of pubs in other towns, especially in Leeds. Whilst Halifax's pubs were full on weekend evenings in the early 1990s, Leeds was a ghost town after the shops closed, something that really surprised me when we went there for our Portman Christmas party in early 1992. There were only a handful of pubs in the city centre and many of them weren't that great although there were some exceptions. The Scarborough Hotel saw occasional pilgrimages to sample its great Tetley and the wonderfully historic Whitelocks is a Leeds institution that is easy to miss in its almost hidden location down an alley off Briggate reflecting its 18th century origins.

Then from the mid-1990s as the city reinvented itself economically as the leading financial centre outside London, transformation soon followed.

Redundant old wharves were redeveloped, red light districts were replaced with cafés and bistros, the Victorian shopping arcades were refurbished and Harvey Nichols arrived. The city centre became home to thousands of new apartments and new bars and restaurants followed in their slipstream. It was new, vibrant, trendy and stylish and people went there to try something new and different rather than the same old pubs of Halifax.

A bit further away, Manchester went through an even more spectacular transformation which accelerated in the aftermath of the IRA bomb in the Summer of 1996. Even lowly Huddersfield became more attractive with new and interesting pubs and bars opening. Nearby Bradford never quite managed it for years as city leaders squabbled and procrastinated for years about the direction to take. Instead, young hipsters and entrepreneurs did their own thing and there is now a thriving craft beer based revival in a small corner just outside the city centre which is doing remarkably well.

Halifax is trying. Entrepreneurs are starting to open some small, nice venues based on selling quality products in a nice environment. There are some terrific restaurants just out of the town centre in Dean Clough, far enough away from the marauding drunks that still populate the town centre at the weekend. I hope these new ventures succeed and that they draw in a crowd that replaces those that want to drink cheap Fosters and fight. The overall decline over the last twenty years has been startling and will continue unless places can raise their game. There are some nice places to go, but the days of dozens of packed pubs selling great beer have sadly gone, and they won't be coming back.

8 READING TIME

The contrast between Sunderland and Reading Universities could not have been greater. Sunderland was a haphazard collection of buildings in varying states of repair dotted around the town. Some departments, including where I was in the School of Business, had found themselves struggling with the increased student intake. More students equalled more money but it took several weeks of chaos before the timetable settled down. There was even a meeting called in the main screen of the town's cinema one afternoon given that it was the only auditorium big enough to accommodate everyone. Frazzled tutors tried heroically to explain things and sort things out.

By contrast, Reading was a long-established university on a sprawling and beautiful green campus on a hill a mile or so out of the town centre. There were hundreds of acres of open space and woods with a large limes-disease ridden lake in the middle. Many of the numerous halls of residence were dotted around the periphery of the campus and it was a lovely environment to live and study in, though I was to do more living than studying. I couldn't believe my luck getting a place there considering that so many of the other students that were starting with me as eighteen and nineteen year olds had got there through working hard to get dazzling 'A' level results. Somehow, I had persuaded them to accept me as a mature student based on work experience and with one year at undergraduate level under my belt.

I quickly settled into my hall of residence, Wessex, which was one of many on campus unchanged since they were built in the 1960s. My tiny room contained a glorified camp bed, a desk and a wardrobe along with some psychedelic curtains in front of a rickety window. There were few luxuries and the showers and toilets were a lengthy walk down two corridors.

A long way from Halifax and eighteen months since we left the Portman, Phil arrived in the Thames Valley. Within no time, we were carrying on where we left off. I was an irresponsible student and he could enjoy a second student experience with his shift-based job allowing him plenty of time to head down the M4 to Reading to blow off steam and drink cheap student beer.

We started as we meant to go on with Freshers' Week whilst he waited for the start date for his new job. I didn't bother with many of the events that were organised and instead Phil and I did our own thing. We went to the off licence to see what 'continental' lager was on offer, that is lager with an ABV of 5% or more. We were established ale drinkers but we were prepared to drink decent canned lager and decent meant nothing under 5% ABV was considered because weak lagers just had no taste. We didn't touch the 'cooking lager' mainstream brands, the likes of Carling, Carlsberg and Fosters which was a contrast to our choice of 'session' beers in the pub that were generally no stronger than 4% ABV (I think Tetley was around 3.6% ABV at the time).

We would get a 'slab' (twenty-four 500ml cans) and take it back to my room. There, we would talk nonsense and put the world to rights listening to music. In that first week we were listening to lots of Pearl Jam because we were big fans and their excellent second album *Vs* had just been released. Once we had demolished the slab we would then wobble out of Wessex Hall and across to Students' Union in the centre of campus for a few more. This was quite an achievement after twelve cans of lager each but somehow we managed it.

All the halls of residence had their own bar. Some of them were far better than others and most of them were better than the Wessex bar which was just a small corner room. In the early days, it was busy with nervous looking people having awkward conversations with each other about what 'A' levels they got but after the first couple of weeks it got quieter and quieter. It wasn't for us and even without the nervous Freshers, it wasn't very appealing. Being such a small room and with us usually being so loaded, the chances of making high profile idiots out of ourselves were quite high and so we thought it better to go elsewhere and blend more discreetly into the crowd.

Wessex was a particularly boring and serious hall that year. There were lots of shy retiring types, quiet overseas students and people who did lots of studying. They were never seen out and about, apart from joining the queue for the telephone booths to phone home each night. My corridor was one of the few that did get lively and once Phil had started work I finally had chance to find out who my fun-loving, beer-drinking neighbours were.

One good thing about Wessex was that it was fully catered. It made the fees more expensive than a self-catering hall, but it was nice to be cooked for three times a day. It was particularly beneficial at breakfast time because there was always bacon and eggs which helped with the terrible hangovers that usually accompanied some of the early starts, particularly when faced with the brutal two-hour accounting lecture at 9am on Monday mornings and the 9am accounting seminar on Fridays. The Friday seminar came after a big student night, in fact the only student night in the town, in the long-gone nightclub Washington Heights. Saturdays were also a highlight for post-beer feeding, especially as breakfast was usually missed. The main meal was called afternoon tea and it was served earlier in the afternoon than on other days of the week. It almost always involved lasagne, chips and mugs of tea poured out of huge, battered metal teapots that looked like they had been in the kitchen since the hall was built. It always hit the spot.

Parties and informal gatherings were held regularly and it was surprising how many people could cram into one of the tiny student bedrooms. Music, cheap canned lager and understanding neighbours were all that were needed. There were occasional early trips to the local pubs but none of them were anything special. The College Arms on Wokingham Road billed itself as a student pub but on the few occasions that we ventured down, we never saw any in there. It wasn't a great pub and, being quite lazy, it was a bit of a trek from campus where there was cheaper beer available. On the other side of campus was the Queen's Head on Christchurch Road. This was a town and gown pub with two separate areas, one for locals and one for students, but it was generally populated by some of the loud public-school prats that gravitated to certain courses at Reading and it was mostly avoided for the three years. Plus, it was on the opposite side of campus and if the College Arms was a bit far, the Queen's Head was more than double the distance. In that first year, entertainment revolved around either amusing ourselves or going to the Students' Union. It wasn't a great Students' Union and was quite small given the size of the campus, but there were two bars and there would always be someone in that you knew. The beer was relatively cheap although I remember being surprised at paying £1.40 for the basic lager, Coors, given the below £1 prices that I had paid in Sunderland.

Wednesday was the big student night at 'the Union' and if you could stomach the lengthy queue in the early days, a lively evening was almost always guaranteed with a full house, lots of beer and a disco with all the predictable student tunes. Traditionally, there were no lectures on Wednesday afternoons in the more old-fashioned universities because this time was designated for sports, of which only a small number of students played. This meant that most of us had a free afternoon on Wednesdays.

The sports clubs started their post-match boozing in the various clubhouses before they headed to the Union for priority access and more of their tedious sports club macho nonsense (and the girls' clubs could be just as badly behaved). There were plenty of braying red-faced toffs in their sports club uniform acting liked they owned the place but the overwhelming number of people in there on Wednesdays were just there for a big booze up. It was a busy, noisy, sweaty evening where hundreds of people milled around the various bars and the disco. During the rest of the week, apart from Friday, there wasn't much going on although they did try to put on some bands. It wasn't on the regular university circuit for bands at the time and it did trade off the fact that U2 had played there (admittedly in 1982). Blur had also performed there in 1990 before they broke through the following year.

We entertained ourselves in our rooms or the corridor's communal area, went to the Union and even started to venture into town and we had a great time together, sometimes too much of a good time with at least one written warning from the bursar to the whole corridor concerning noise. There was a great social life with great friends on tap, the workload wasn't particularly demanding (though I should have worked far harder than I did) and I was also taking the train regularly to go and see Phil for more beer where he was living.

The first year came around far too quickly and in no time it was approaching the end of the Summer term. We had to vacate our rooms in the Christmas and Easter holidays and I went back to Halifax where I picked up some hours at the Portman. I wasn't to return during the Summer and the Easter of 1994 was to be the very last time I pulled a pint at the Portman. It was a place that had given me so much pleasure. It introduced me to a great lifelong friend, really opened me up to the world of beer and pubs and did wonders for my self-confidence, but I wasn't to return.

I had the chance to return to France for a third consecutive year having done a shorter stint between leaving Sunderland and starting at Reading, but decided against it and instead I decided to address my long-held fascination with America and I headed across the Atlantic as part of the British Universities North America Club (BUNAC) scheme. I spent eight weeks of penury working as a driver on a children's camp in Lake George, a four-hour drive north of New York. I had never flown long-haul before and I was terrified on my Virgin flight to JFK, not leaving my seat once. I hadn't yet discovered the benefits of several pints of strong lager in the airport terminal to help with the nerves.

The camp was in a beautiful location, very rural with miles and miles of mountains, forests and lakes. It might have been pretty, but there was very little to do with it being miles from the nearest community, never mind town. The camp was isolated and the pay was poor but I had it better than most because as service staff we shared our own bunkhouse whereas the camp counsellors had to share with their student charges. Plus, I got to get out and about a lot more because being the minibus driver entailed driving the kids to events and competitions as well as errand running into the quaint, but very much red-neck, local towns.

With the camp's isolation, there was very, very little beer. The counsellors went to the nearest town on their night off for a few beers and they then crammed as many as they could into a motel room, grateful to have a night away from a wooden cabin full of kids. There was a bar in the town that had a liberal approach to serving under age foreign workers (the legal drinking age there being twenty-one). They got away with it for most of the Summer until the police busted the bar with only a week to go until the end of camp. Some delicate negotiations between the camp director and the local police department kept them out of jail and the charge sheets were taken home to be framed as souvenirs of a very close shave.

The beery shortfall over the Summer was quickly corrected on returning to Reading. Five of us from Wessex Hall rented a house on London Road in the 'colourful' area of Cemetery Junction. The house was awful, like something from *The Young Ones* and it was sandwiched between a motorbike shop and, allegedly, one of Reading's more notorious drug dealing houses, though we never saw or heard anything unusual. It was just along the road from chip shops, kebab shops, off licences and a couple of grotty pubs and was an ideal location. There was the Granby pub which was a dive but student friendly and the Jack of Both Sides which was also a dive and not so student friendly. Apart from Wednesday night at the Students' Union which a couple of us liked, the focus became more on discovering new places to go and things to do rather than going up onto campus. With our own house, we could entertain ourselves with having much more space. We could also make more noise given that there weren't any diligent Malaysian students down the corridor trying to study.

What did change in that second year starting in September 1994 was music. Music was to become synonymous with beer to us as Phil and I rode a beer-fuelled wave of possibly the greatest eighteen months in British music since the last greatest eighteen months in British music. Think Madchester in 1989/90 or punk in 1976/77 for starters, not that we were old enough to remember that. We were so lucky. It probably was and will be the last great period in music. There hasn't been one since. There's still good music around but none with the star quality of those 'big' bands of the past. I look at festival line ups and almost weep. Justin Bieber at the V Festival? Really? Phil and I were lucky enough to have been from the generation that had experienced the mega artists of the 1980s, the Madchester scene, Thames Valley 'shoe-gazing' and then the Seattle-led invasion of American rock from 1991 until a heroin-laden Kurt Cobain blew his brains out in April 1994. By then the hype and hysteria around Nirvana had reached silly levels. Cobain's especially violent and depressing death was a huge shock. A musical gap was left that was about to be filled in spectacular fashion.

At the Summer camp in New York I discovered the local college radio station which had a terrific alternative playlist as well as heavily promoting the bands that were appearing on the Lollapalooza tour as it came through the state. There were plenty of names I'd never heard of who hadn't and didn't make their way across the Atlantic. One of those that did was a quirky new band called Weezer whose *Sweater Song* was getting a lot of play on the station ahead of their debut album that came out later that year. There were also some lads from Wigan getting a lot of airplay. They were in a band I had vaguely heard of but didn't really know called The Verve. They were amazing and I became hooked, buying their 1993 debut *A Storm in Heaven* as soon as I got back from the States.

Returning from America, the space left by the bursting of the Seattle bubble was about to be filled by home-grown talent, and it was fantastic. It didn't take long for someone to give it a stupid name and, like the 'grunge' label applied to the Seattle bands, 'Britpop' was the awful moniker attached to these British bands that were to dominate over the next couple of years. Oasis had been making noises that year and in late 1994 their debut album *Definitely Maybe* arrived with a bang just in time for our return to Reading.

Other bands that had been around for some time were also starting to get traction including Blur who had surprised a lot of people, including previously non-Blur fans like myself, by releasing the brilliant *Parklife* earlier in the year which had gained momentum and many converts over the subsequent months. British music was in the ascendancy after a couple of years of American domination and there was so much more good stuff to come.

Much as Phil and I had enjoyed our music, it was confined to listening to CDs and drinking beer. Our love of music and beer was about to step up to a whole new level when, inspired by all the great new music that was around, we started going to see bands live rather than just listening to them. Beer was an intrinsic part of these evenings.

It all started in surprising fashion at the end of 1994 by getting tickets for the Stone Roses. Radio One was still contemporary and a trailblazer for all this great music that was coming out. Phil was off shift one day and listening to the radio when he heard the announcement that they were launching a tour at the end of 1994 to promote *Second Coming*, their pretty good but ultimately disappointing (compared to the first) second album. I caught the train to Paddington and we met up for a few beers in central London before heading south to the Brixton Academy. A few more beers seemed like the right thing to do and so we called in to the Wetherspoon's on the High Street. There I had my first experience of UV lights in the gents' toilets which puzzled me until I later discovered that UV light was used to deter intravenous drug use because users would be unable to see their veins. I'd led a sheltered life in Halifax.

Suitably refreshed, we then walked down the road to the Academy and used our sharp elbows to get to the front where we had a great evening. It wasn't a bad first gig to go to together and we became hooked. It was great timing because the following year Britpop went bonkers. It was such a great time to be alive, free from the constraints of work and being a student where you could really take advantage of everything that was going on. It seemed that almost every week there was a new CD to buy. There were new albums by Radiohead, The Boo Radleys, Black Grape, Elastica, Sleeper, Supergrass, Teenage Fanclub, Paul Weller, Echobelly, The Verve, Blur, Oasis, The Charlatans and Pulp to name but a few. There were also all the other less high-profile bands that didn't quite 'make it' in the same way. One of my favourites was Moose, but they never broke through. There was a lot of time spent in the Virgin Megastore and HMV in Reading town centre followed by a few beers and, in those pre-internet days, a browse through the adverts at the back of the *New Musical Express* to see what the upcoming gigs were before going home to phone Ticketmaster.

Pre-gig beers were compulsory and we settled on either the Wetherspoon's on Leicester Square for an easy place to meet and cheap beer or the Intrepid Fox in Soho which was a bit more 'edgy' and no matter how many times I went, I always struggled to find it. I believe it is now closed and a burger bar.

After a few early drinks, it was then on to the venue to drink industrial quantities of overpriced continental strength lager from plastic glasses. There were lots and lots of gigs and what we thought would be a highlight in the Autumn of 1995 was one weekend where we saw Radiohead at Brixton Academy one night followed by Oasis at Earls Court the next. Radiohead were brilliant. Their first album and the hit single *Creep* were very much pre-Britpop and had passed me by at the time, but I had seen them support R.E.M at Milton Keynes Bowl in the Summer of 1995 (third on the bill below the Cranberries). I was hugely impressed at their big, tight sound and the show at Brixton didn't disappoint. It was a loud, powerful show that sounded even better in the confines of a relatively small venue compared to a huge outdoor arena.

Although Blur arguably went on to win the war, Oasis were the Britpop winners towards the end of 1995 and they were the biggest, most hyped band in the country after the release of *(What's The Story) Morning Glory?* The next night at Earls' Court was a such a disappointment. It was OK, but it certainly wasn't great. It didn't help that we were stuck up in the seats rather than our preferred location on the floor, but they were the only tickets that were available. We couldn't drink the beer that we wanted to due to the shambolic bar arrangements which meant lengthy delays and we never bothered going to see them again. They had their moments with a handful of good songs, but I still think they were very overrated.

Perhaps the greatest, or certainly the most memorable, gig was one of the earliest ones that we went to. The legendary Shaun Ryder had been doing his stuff for years before Britpop. The Happy Mondays dated from the mid-1980s and they peaked in 1989/1990 with the *Madchester Rave On EP* followed by the innovative and commercially successful *Pils 'n' Thrills and Bellyaches* album. Implosion had followed not long afterwards in a crack-fuelled disaster in the Caribbean supposedly recording their next album.

Amazingly, not only did he manage to put a new band together a couple of years later, but he had also somehow managed to write some great tunes and get a record deal. The result was the astonishing *It's Great When You're Straight...Yeah!* which was released to rave reviews. I thought the reviewer in the magazine *Vox* that I read regularly at the time had made a mistake when I saw the 9/10 score from their review, but they were not alone in their view. Other papers and magazines gave it similarly great reviews and scores. Based on the reviews, I bought it and on the first play instantly agreed with all of them. It was a terrific record with a great vibe, catchy tunes and cheeky lyrics. Phil and I both agreed that it was something special and he was someone who had never been a Happy Mondays fan. We got straight on the phone to Ticketmaster to get tickets for their London show which was to be in unfamiliar territory in north London at the Kentish Town Forum.

We had already done some exploring of some of the pubs around Camden Lock and the market, though I never made it to The Good Mixer, supposedly the spiritual home of Britpop. After meeting in the Wetherspoon's on Leicester Square, we headed north. We didn't know Kentish Town at all and so we just found a conveniently placed pub near to the venue for some more pre-gig beers before heading across the road to the Forum. We got some beers from the bar at the back of the room and from there it was easy to see the stage given that it was only a small venue. The place soon filled up and the anticipation mounted with no one really knowing what to expect given that it was a new band on their first tour. Plus, and Shaun Ryder's unpredictability was well known.

There were probably around a thousand people in there but when the lights went down and Shaun Ryder swaggered on to the stage, it felt like that there were three times that number. There was an explosion of noise, a surge towards the stage and plastic glasses of lager (hopefully it was lager) went flying. The crowd got into the groove of the opening song within seconds of the first notes being played. We swilled our beer and piled into the crowd, quickly muscling our way to the front.

While Bez was doing his freaky dancing thing, Shaun Ryder shuffled around the stage in a white baggy jumper with an enormous, chunky gold chain round his neck and very expensive looking crocodile leather shoes. We got right up to the barrier and with only a very shallow security pit at the front of the stage, we were close enough to see the laminated sheets with song lyrics which he periodically knelt to read from. In front of the microphone stand were two girls leaning on the barrier getting jostled and battered by the surging crowd and they were clearly struggling. We noticed this and seeing that they were in difficulty, we did what we thought was an honourable thing of putting our arms around each other with my left arm and Phil's right arm gripping the barrier therefore creating a little pocket of space for them to enjoy the show as we absorbed the crowd around us.

We were enjoying the show, we were in the groove and we were off our faces on the lager when what happened next made sure that this remained the most memorable of all the gigs that we went to. As Black Grape belted out the songs, one of the girl's bra clasps popped, with absolutely no interference from us I should say. It was quite a sight. I have no idea how it happened and with a limited knowledge of these things, I just assume it was completely random. Luckily, thanks to our efforts her friend had a small amount of space in which to try and correct the wardrobe malfunction but even so, despite Phil and I giving them some space and protection, there was still lots of jostling. It was dark and they had also no doubt had a few lagers. It took ages to bring the contents under control with ever increasing amounts of flesh being exposed as the friend struggled to perform a relatively simple task in rather difficult conditions. We were completely distracted from the show on stage to the show going on right in front of us. After what seemed like an age, the friend finally succeeded. The relief could be seen on both of their faces and we all continued to enjoy the rest of the gig, Phil and I both picking our jaws up off the floor and exchanging looks of bewilderment and smirking at the turn of events.

They were grateful for our help both with the general protection and the help this provided during the bra incident. When the show finished, the whole crowd seemed completely buoyed up after what had been a great concert as they slowly filtered out into the night. The four of us were left nervously looking at each other. We had come to the show with no real plan about doing anything afterwards and normally we just headed home. They certainly had the look that they were waiting for us to ask what they were doing after the show, or at least say something now that we finally able to hear each other.

Phil and I were both wired from a great show and lots of lager and looked at each other and simultaneously said 'beer!' and we turned and headed off to the exit. We never even thought to ask the girls if they wanted to join us. Off we went, and instead of a rare chance to chat and maybe go for a drink with attractive young women, we acted like morons, dashing off back into central London to drink yet more beer. We headed to the legendary, if by this stage somewhat grotty, Marquee Club. At the time, they did an indie all-nighter at the weekend and we lasted well into the night, stumbling out on to Charing Cross road in the dawn light. Not long afterwards the iconic venue closed and it became a Wetherspoon's. The girls must have thought we were idiots and there was absolutely no doubt that we were.

With the success of Britpop, even Reading University could attract moderately successful bands. Forgetting Carter and the Unstoppable Sex Machine who played in the first year and an unsuccessful hosting of specialist flavour indie band Cud which had to be downgraded to the smaller room due to poor ticket sales, the Students' Union did manage to attract some decent bands in late 1995 and early 1996. This meant that we didn't always have to go into London and Phil came down to Reading for an afternoon in the pub before heading to the gig. Apart from a dreadful performance by Echobelly where singer Sonya Madan had a bit of a strop with the crowd who weren't overly appreciative of what seemed like a below par performance, there were some great gigs by Cast, The Charlatans, The Boo Radleys and The Bluetones. For the Bluetones, still one of my favourite of the Britpop bands, we got tickets 0001 and 0002 from the box office.

What we didn't do in that Britpop era was go to a festival. My housemates went to Glastonbury 1995 where not only did it not rain, but it was baking hot. It was also still in the days when you could pay ne'er-do-wells to get you over or under the fence for a few quid which an estimated twenty thousand people did. The Stone Roses were due to headline but the guitarist had broken his arm and so their place was taken by Pulp who delivered a legendary performance. Oasis headlined the first night and The Cure the last.

Neither did we ever make it to the Reading Festival which was a bit poor considering that it was just down the road. Held over the August bank holiday weekend, the town would be full of people drinking, getting provisions (which meant clearing the supermarket shelves of beer) and finding a half decent loo in the pubs and shops before drifting back to the festival site later in the afternoon. Nirvana's appearances in 1991 and especially in 1992 when they headlined had gone down in folklore. Perhaps surprisingly for the Britpop dominated era, the line-up in 1995 was dominated by great overseas acts like Smashing Pumpkins, Bjork, Neil Young, Foo Fighters, Soundgarden, Pavement and Mudhoney amongst other big hitters as well as a host of second tier Britpop bands like Shed Seven, Gene, Boo Radleys and Cast. Even the Bluetones featured on the second stage despite only having released a couple of singles at the time. I didn't go because by this stage I was back working in a pub and, at the time, three twelve-hour shifts over the weekend seemed like a better idea than spending money I didn't have going to the festival. There would always be next year I thought. That was a mistake.

9 WORKING IN PUBS - 2

I admit it: I quite like Wetherspoon's. Or should I say, I don't mind them, some of them at least. I don't like them as much as I used to and standards have slipped a lot over the years, at least in the ones that I have been to recently. I've been to some nice ones, but I am finding that they can be increasingly hit and miss, often more of a miss. For a chain that supposedly champions real ale so much, it is common to walk in to a pub with a lot of pumps, all with 'coming soon' labels on them and nothing but Doom Bar and Abbot Ale available. Too many seem to suffer with a limited range of beers, badly served beer, dirty tables and surly staff although perhaps I am being unfair given my sample size.

They divide opinion and there are plenty of people that like to sneer at the pubs and the people that go to them, blaming Wetherspoon's for many of the ills of the pub trade, but they have found their place in the market, if 9am drinkers is one of the markets that you want. With a Wetherspoon's you generally know what you're going to get and at what kind of price.

At the time of the pub tube map in 1995, they were still a few years away from arriving in Halifax. Now there are now two in the town centre as well as one each in nearby Sowerby Bridge and Brighouse. In the mid-1990s there were barely any outside the M25. Once they made that move outside their traditional border of the London Orbital, their growth and spread was rapid. They are now part of the high street in towns and cities the length and breadth of the country, but when I first encountered them it was very much a London thing.

It should come as no surprise that Phil was involved in this discovery. The first Wetherspoon's experience was in the less than salubrious west London suburb of Hounslow in early 1994. Hounslow was a cheap place to live if you were on a budget and could tolerate the relentless noise of aircraft taking off and landing at nearby Heathrow every couple of minutes. Phil was lodging there having recently started his new job and he was excited one day to tell me that he had found a half decent pub (a rarity for Hounslow) where they sold beer for 89p per pint.

This early discovery was the Moon Under Water on Staines Road which had opened a couple of years earlier. It was unspectacular but a huge improvement on the other grim pubs we had found whilst exploring Hounslow. Phil had done a little research since discovering this new source of cheap beer and he told me about their principles of no music or fruit machines and that many of them were called the Moon Under Water or variations of in reference to George Orwell's 1946 essay describing his mythical 'perfect' pub. Phil railed at the no music policy but this was overlooked given the lack of other options and the competitive prices.

Fast forward to September and I was back in Reading after returning from America ready to start second year life in Cemetery Junction. I was wandering through Reading town centre and spotted a large new looking pub across from the town hall. Thinking that it was about time I got some part time work, I wandered in and asked to speak to the manager. With the impeccable timing that has evaded me in so many other career decisions, I was in the right place at the right time and I found myself as a newly employed J D Wetherspoon barman at the recently opened Monks' Retreat. At the time of walking in I hadn't even realised it was a Wetherspoon's and I didn't make the connection with the cheap beer pub in Hounslow from earlier in the year.

To me it was just a big, decent-looking pub and it was a vast improvement on the rest of Reading's town centre pubs which at the time were awful. We had explored most of them, usually only once, and I wouldn't have wanted to work in any of them. We didn't even want to drink in most of them. Little did I know at the time but I was at the vanguard of a revolution that would see the company go from a small London-centric chain to nationwide dominance in a few short years. The Monks' Retreat was a pioneer in being one of the first of the chain's pubs to be opened outside the M25. As a result, the spotlight was on it and mullet haired boss Tim Martin called in on numerous occasions to see how things were going.

It was converted from a former electrical shop and it had no architectural merit or charm whatsoever unlike some of their later, more ambitious additions to the chain. It was like other shop fronts, blending into the high street with large floor to ceiling windows although they did make an effort at presentation with plenty of hanging baskets. Inside, it conformed to the standard Wetherspoon's formula of the time. There was no television, no music or any fruit machines. The decor was dark wood and blue carpets and staff wore white shirts and black trousers and - heaven forbid for a former Portman employee - a tie.

It was run by a fabulous Irish couple called Eugene and Shirley. Eugene wasn't that much older than me and rarely seemed to smile which was hardly surprising given the phenomenal hours that he had to work, but when he did he was hilarious. His laid-back approach masked someone who was acutely aware of the bottom line and who was really on top of the business. We even had a connection with Halifax because he had worked on the huge extension to the head office of the Halifax Building Society in the late 1980s. With the end of the project and the downturn in the building trade in the early 1990s recession, he had to explore other opportunities and, after serving his apprenticeship in some of the company's smaller London venues, he found himself running this flagship project in Reading.

There was no doubt that Eugene ran a tight ship. There was an established group of full and part time staff, many of whom had been there since the pub opened earlier in the year. The start of the new student year brought an influx of new starters, many of whom would be whittled out after being closely observed by Eugene. He knew exactly what was going on and even though he was rarely behind the bar, he was almost always on the premises with maybe a couple of hours off in the afternoon after the lunchtime rush had ended.

There were two bars in the pub which was a large 'L' shaped floor space. The first bar was immediately on the left after walking through the doors. With some tall tables in the middle and booths around the edge, this was more of a drinking bar but deeper inside the building after going up some steps there were larger booths and a much larger bar hidden around the corner with a food ordering point and the kitchen. The upper area was designed with eating in mind and it was a no-smoking area years ahead of its time. It reminded me of a larger, cleaner and more modern Portman with the shape of the pub and the lack of natural light.

It was dark, but it was an improvement on its Hounslow stable mate and was a massive improvement on the other pubs in Reading at the time. The town centre was truly dire for pubs when I arrived in 1993. It had a good selection of shops including some of the big names but it was terrible if you wanted to go for a pint. I just can't imagine where people went after work for a drink because it was a decent sized town with some big employers there. The town centre had perhaps half a dozen pubs and almost all of them were dark, dirty, dreary and depressing with few customers using them.

The only one we liked, initially at least, was the Hobgoblin on Broad Street which we found and discovered not long after it had been renovated and renamed after 150 years as the London Tavern. It was very much a real ale pub. Sadly it was run by some deeply unpleasant real ale enthusiasts with scratty beards and dirty t-shirts that didn't quite stretch over their guts to tuck in to their equally grubby jeans. They typified everything that was wrong with real ale enthusiasts and they conformed perfectly to the negative stereotype many people had of them. The first time we went in I ordered whatever beer I was having. One of the group was only eighteen and not long arrived at university. He was very inexperienced about pubs given his boarding school education deep in the countryside and when he ordered, he innocently asked for a pint of Fosters. That's what he had drunk on the few occasions that he had been to the pub and he thought nothing of it. Cue sneering and ridicule from behind the bar. It wasn't even 'banter' or 'jokey,' it was nasty and it was delivered in a 'how dare you come into *this* pub and order *that?*' He did actually say 'We don't sell that shit in here' as part of his diatribe. I don't disagree with his view on Fosters but it was a bad attitude to have and it is not uncommon amongst some real ale purists working behind bars.

On another occasion, we went into the back which was a little warren of wooden booths. Either the whole area was no-smoking or half of it was I can't quite remember, but we were definitely in the no-smoking area. Some lads were just leaving as we arrived and they had moved an ashtray onto a no-smoking table and had smoked a cigarette. We were about to sit at the table they had vacated. The barman, I'm not sure if it was the same one, came to collect glasses, saw the ashtray and instantly launched into us about smoking in a no-smoking area, even though none of us were smoking and we'd only just walked in to the area after ordering our beers from him. There would have been no time to walk the few steps to the table and smoke a cigarette. Again, it was bad attitude and very confrontational. If he had spoken like that with a group of lads feistier than us it could have *easily* have resulted in him receiving a punch in the face. It was a shame because it was a decent pub with decent beer but two visits and two bad experiences was enough to put us off. I didn't go back in until 2013.

With one decent real ale pub (despite the staff), and one half decent 'wine bar' type place there wasn't much competition in Reading at the time. With the mainly dark and dirty pubs in the town centre as competition, the Monks' Retreat was a big, modern, clean pub without sticky floors that you could go to for an affordable drink and something to eat. It attracted a mix of customers and you were just as welcome if you had done a day's work on a building site or if you had come from an office.

The prices also helped its popularity. The discounted Youngers Scotch Bitter that we had drunk in Hounslow was still on the bar in Reading at 99p. That was the standard year-round price, but in the New Year it was discounted to 89p, in February to 79p and finally in March to 69p. Theakstons Best Bitter and Theakstons XB were also served and, to my surprise, were served with northern style sparklers. The Best Bitter was £1.35 which was comparable to northern prices at the time and the slightly stronger XB was £1.49. As a gesture to the local brewery, Courage and their huge Worton Grange brewery at the side of the M4 (which closed in 2010), there was also Courage Directors' bitter. Guinness was £1.59, McEwan's lager was £1.35 and Kronenbourg 1664 was £1.85. The McEwan's was cheaper than lager at the Students' Union and it wasn't served in a plastic glass.

It was a busy pub, popular with workers, shoppers and price conscious students and pensioners all using it. I worked almost as hard on a busy lunchtime as I did at the Portman on an evening. The volume of food that came out of the tiny kitchen with its multinational Peruvian, Croatian and local staff was astonishing. Working 12 noon until 2pm was a hectic shift during the week and it went on all day on Saturdays with the shopping crowd coming into eat at more staggered intervals. Friday and Saturday nights were relentless. Even after the busy weekends in the Portman, I had never been in a pub with so many people in it before and although it seems tiny compared to the mega pubs Wetherspoon's went on to open, it was far bigger than anything in Halifax. It was a place everyone wanted to go to given the lack of other options. On Fridays, the day time crowd gave way to the post work crowd which started coming in from mid-afternoon and whilst some stayed, they mainly gave way to the night-time crowd in a relentless stream of people. It was hard, hard work with people yelling at the bar and waiting three or four deep no matter how quickly we tried to serve them.

When it was all done for the night there was then the vast amounts of stocking up to do, bringing up box after box of beers, mixers and soft drinks from the cellar which was a long walk and a lot of stairs from the top bar especially. The weekend crowd weren't interested in Youngers Scotch Bitter at 99p per pint. They wanted bottles of Fosters Ice and Miller Genuine Draft. With Fosters Ice especially, we went through pallet loads of the stuff.

The Portman was a holiday camp in comparison. Working at the Monks there were no pull through snakebites or any four-pint half hour breaks. You couldn't even have a staff drink when you were working, not that there was much chance to drink them. Plus, getting a drink bought for you was a real rarity. They weren't a generous crowd like they were up north.

We were uniformed corporate machines in a much more organised and structured environment than I'd known at the Portman. Rotas were strict and individual shifts even had their own rota, especially at busy food times so that you would have time allocated to do 'the floor' which meant no serving behind the bar. Instead, you were responsible for clearing plates back into the kitchen and glasses into the wash area and back out on to the shelves. The glasses were stacked in the crates they were washed in to save valuable unloading time.

There was data published in the staff room that showed how much each person had taken per shift and the rate of takings and transactions per hour.

It was the kind of thing that could be taken several ways. Some, the slackers, saw it negatively as snooping but it was an effective way of showing who the slackers were in a very public way. Some of us, mainly the blokes, took it as a challenge and it got super competitive, almost like a league table. On weekend evenings that competitiveness was ratcheted up because at the end of the shift on Friday and Saturday nights, a 'man of the match' for each bar was chosen with the winner getting a free pint. It was a lot of effort for one measly pint.

If you worked hard, arrived on time, didn't blob your shift at the last minute and got on with the job with the right attitude, Eugene looked after you. You would get time off when you needed it, first choice for extra shifts and a free pint every now and again. If you didn't work hard or have the right attitude, Eugene would rarely sack you, but he would manoeuvre people out that weren't pulling their weight.

One notoriously one-speed, sour faced bar man who had been there for some time questioned Eugene after hours one night in front of all the staff as we relaxed with a drink. He asked why new starters seemed to be getting the pick of shifts and he was finding it hard to get extras. Eugene said that this wasn't really the time and place for this conversation and that he should talk to him privately another time. When he pursued the point, Eugene said again to come and speak to him later. When he persisted a third time, Eugene very calmly said that maybe it was because the new guys had a smile on their face and didn't mope around the place with a face like a smacked arse. There was instant silence and everyone was open-mouthed waiting to see what was going to happen next. It was quite a put down, but delivered in his ever so gentle Irish voice. He didn't raise his voice, shout or lose his temper. The guy got right in Eugene's face and said, 'Nice car outside EUGENE' and stormed out. Eugene remained calm, watched him walk out and waited for the door to close before saying to the group with a puzzled expression on his face 'I don't even own a car,' which was true, to roaring laughter. Whether he did over some innocent bloke's car, I don't know but I doubt it. I don't think he had it in him and he was a nice lad, just very dreary. Sadly, his girlfriend was part of the assembled group. She was lovely, goodness knows why she was with him, and she was embarrassed and angry. She hurriedly collected her things and followed him out of the pub close to tears with a beetroot coloured face. We never saw either of them in the place again.

The opening staff soon faded away, such is the nature of turnover of staff in big, busy pubs. More and more students came in and there was flexibility on both sides because four hour shifts weren't too demanding and it created a sizeable, flexible group of people to fill holes in the roster. Plus, with four hour shifts, they didn't need to give you a break. When you were accepted as a good, hard working barman (or woman) and part of the team, you were looked after. I got a good feed from the kitchen when working the frequent double (and often triple) shifts and often on shifts when I wasn't eligible for food if there was something about to go out of date in the kitchen. I even cheekily got the use of the bar towel washing machine (we didn't have a washing machine in the house) until abuse by others made Eugene impose a ban. It even got to the point where Eugene and I would play squash at the university sports centre each week on his afternoon off which, I am led to believe, fired up his endorphins for when he got home. It was just about the only change of scene he got outside the pub because in the early days the hours he worked were relentless.

I became well established there. It was a good crowd of co-workers and we did lots together socially. The main reason for getting work was to fund the student social life and, instead, I found a whole new social life that needed funding. We were having a blast, working and going out together. The Summer of 1995 was baking hot, Britpop was in full swing and Reading was ever so slowly evolving. An old bank across the road was converted into a decent pub called the Old Society, one of the old biker pubs around the corner received a much-needed refurbishment and a decent pub opened in the nearby railway station. We were spending more time in the town than on the campus and a lot of it in the Monks thanks to their prices.

As Reading was changing, so were customer tastes that Spring and Summer. The first trend we noticed was people coming in and asking if we sold Caffreys. We had never heard of it until the pub on the station started selling it. Word got out and people were going to the station specifically to drink it and then wandering into the town to see if there was anywhere else selling it. Little did we know at the time but this coincided with its relaunch by Bass in 1994 although its heritage went back to Dublin in the late 18th century. It was a 'smooth' keg style product and was quite drinkable, especially for northern exiles that missed a creamy head on a pint. We went to the station to investigate and it was a refreshing change to drink a beer that was different to the flat Courage on offer in most places around the town. It wasn't cheap and it only took one or two sessions to realise that it needed to be respected because however nice it tasted, it wasn't a session beer. Foolishly, because it was very drinkable, we drank it like a session beer and whether it was the strength (4.8% ABV), the chemicals or both it would result in a fearsome headache if you had too much.

Of much more significance and much more noticeable in the hot weather of 1995 was the number of people coming in and asking, 'Do you sell Hooch?' What on earth was Hooch? Again, we'd never heard of it, but plenty of people had because more and more people were asking for it. It was a product that would signal a substantial change in drinking habits in the 1990s and encourage a whole load of tabloid controversy and publicity as well as the addition of 'alcopop' to the dictionary. Tabloid outrage and publicity; just what a new product needs and the manufacturers were no doubt rubbing their hands with glee as sales grew to over two million bottles per week at its peak. And who was responsible for bringing this to market? None other than Bass, who were also behind Caffreys. Possibly the two biggest new trends in drinking in the mid-1990s were introduced by the legendary Burton beer producer. I couldn't see the appeal myself, although we did foolishly experiment with Hooch shandies at barbeques. A boozy drink that tasted like lemonade in hot weather undoubtedly had its fans, especially amongst women who wanted a long drink but didn't like or want to drink beer. It took a while before Wetherspoon's latched onto this trend and we were soon stocking and selling boxes and boxes of one of the copycat competitors, Two Dogs.

For my third year at university, and my second year at the Monks, I was working twelve-hour shifts on Thursdays and Fridays and as much as I could during the holidays. It was busy and it was fun and it included my twenty fifth birthday where a day out in the pubs of Henley-on-Thames was followed by an evening in a small pub down a side street just outside Reading town centre called the Retreat. This was similar in style to the Big Six in that it was small and in the middle of a row of terraced houses but it did lack all the Big Six's charm, heritage and beer quality. It was very quiet, which was one of the reasons we liked it. It also sold pickled eggs, that beer snack monstrosity that I have a strange and occasional liking for after a belly full of beer though goodness knows why. My mates assumed I would want one as a birthday treat because they thought that all northerners eat pickled eggs and so they bought me one.

The landlord was entering the spirit of things having a laugh and a joke with us given that we had taken over his otherwise empty pub. Correctly sensing that I was far more inebriated than him, he somehow involved me in a pickled egg eating competition. I was merrily eating the eggs, oblivious to the fact that he was distracting me and passing his eggs onto my plate whilst feigning eating his own. He declared me the winner, just as I began with some rather uncomfortable rumblings down below. There then followed a sudden dash to the loo where I projectile vomited an unfeasible amount of undigested pickled eggs, some of which even made it to the target. With that little unpleasantness out of the way, it was back to the Guinness and the remainder of the evening.

A couple of days later I was working at the Monks when a familiar looking face walked in. He didn't seem to have the same sense of recognition that I had but it was my pickled egg eating companion from a few nights earlier. He ordered his drinks and after handing him his change, I sheepishly reminded him who I was and apologised for the pebble-dashed toilet. He glared at me for a second then burst into laughter. He said he wasn't bothered given that we had spent a lot of money and behaved ourselves.

Plus, he said, it wasn't his job to clean the toilet. Not that the Retreat at the time was the kind of pub that paid too much attention to the state of its gents' toilet.

Silly behaviour dominated the third year, even more so than the previous two. Numerous alcohol-related injuries were picked up amongst the house-mates and a lot of fun was had by all, including the 'Hundred Club.' This was a concept brought back by some of the house-mates after an incident packed couple of months in Greece where they tried and generally failed to work over the Summer holidays. The Hundred Club was a good excuse to fill an otherwise dull Sunday afternoon.

The concept seemed simple enough because all it needed was a large bowl which was filled with beer and a plastic 35mm film case each. The contest was to last a hundred minutes and at the strike of each minute, you were to fill your camera case with beer and drink it, then wait for the minute hand to go around again before repeating the process on the next minute and so on for a hundred times. Failure to drink on the strike of a minute meant disqualification. Also, you weren't allowed to go to the toilet once the contest had started without being disqualified. It seemed easy enough because after all, the camera case was tiny. The game started slowly but it didn't take long before the minute hand was coming around quicker and quicker to the point where in the closing stages it was a race to drink a tiny plastic mouthful of beer within a minute. Try it, if you can still find 35mm film cases lying around.

Quitting was not an option and on reaching the hundredth minute there was a race to the downstairs loo at the back of the house with the rest bursting into the back garden to relieve bursting bladders, much to the dismay of the neighbours. Then, it was on to the pub.

Pubs, concerts, Student Unions and slabs of cans in the house, there was a lot of beer drunk over those couple of years in Cemetery Junction. Sadly though, all good things come to an end. It was a real wrench to leave university because it had been such a blast, everything I wanted and more. I even somehow managed to leave with a 2:2 degree. The last couple of weeks involved lots of partying, sometimes two sessions in one day in the wild week after degree results had been received when, after a big night out people woke up on the sofa or the bean bags in the lounge, still felt giddy and tipsy and cracked open the cans and started again for a few hours before some more sleep and going out again at night. It was very hedonistic and not behaviour to be encouraged in anything other than very small doses.

It was also a wrench to leave the pub where I had learned a lot over nearly two years, but not only was I leaving university but I was leaving Reading as well. With a nice parting gift from the Monks, it was on to pastures new. I had pulled no doubt thousands of pints over the previous five years but now, as a graduate, those days were behind me. I vowed never to work behind a bar again and headed back to Halifax, broke and worn out from all the beer. I hung around at my parents for a couple of weeks waiting for a phone call. When it came, it would tell me that my flight was booked to take me to the other side of the world.

10 KOREA MOVE

A rest from beer was long overdue on leaving university, so much so that I didn't even head to the Big Six when I was back in Halifax. I didn't have any money for a start after a particularly silly end to our time at Reading. There was lots of going out and enjoying our last taste of 'freedom' before entering the world of work. It was nice to have some quiet time in Halifax where I was waiting for the confirmation of my flight details to South Korea where I had got a job. For someone needing a rest from beer and three years of student boozing, possibly the worst place to go to was South Korea. There, they loved to drink.

It was hardly the place that I had expected to be starting work after university, but an opportunity presented itself, the pay was good and there were no other offers on the table. I had applied to countless companies that resulted in only two interviews, neither of which were successful, and so when the interview for the job in Korea was offered which was effectively held in a storeroom in the basement of the embassy near the Albert Hall, I was short of options and therefore prepared extra hard. I studied, rehearsed and even taught myself a few words of the language which met with approval. I thought it went well and called for a pint at the first pub I could find on the way back to the Underground.

The confirmation of the job, teaching English in South Korean middle schools, came through within a couple of days and we celebrated in the Fruitbat, an odd little bar that had opened in the heart of the student area on Erleigh Road, a short walk from Cemetery Junction. The salary was comparable with many graduate salaries in the UK, but was tax free and included a rent-free apartment. Towards the end of August I packed my case and headed to London and onwards to Seoul before arriving at the Korea National University of Education for my orientation.

South Korea is a country full of remote natural beauty and crowded cities.

It was a country on the go. Its economy was maturing and it was doing very well, forty years after much of it was flattened during the Korean War. The country's GDP per capita at the start of the 1960s was similar to newly independent African countries but by the 1990s it was a modern, dynamic affluent country. Some people still eked out a living in some ramshackle properties in the cities but more and more old buildings were being razed to be replaced by modern, clean, dull, functional apartment blocks. Even in the poorer countryside, the houses of the poorest farm workers still had solid walls, a roof, running water and electricity. There wasn't much in them beyond a TV and a telephone, but there wasn't the abject poverty and people living in shacks that I was expecting and that is still visible in other growing Asian economies. It was modern, yet very traditional, and I soon fell in love with the place.

I ended up in the far south of the country in the beautiful island and town of Wando, the furthest south you can get before getting on a ferry. It was a small town that hugged the harbour with the rest of the island being sparsely populated and agricultural and it was dominated by a large mountain in the middle. Looking out to sea were dozens of small islands of varying size, many of which were still inhabited and connected with numerous small ferries.

Whilst most teachers chose to head to the cities or large towns, I chose Wando because I wanted to experience the 'real' South Korea, and it couldn't have been any more real than in Wando. After the orientation period, we were shipped out to our new homes which initially for me was an apartment with a picturesque view of the harbour if I ignored the engineering workshop outside my balcony. One of the local teachers took me to my apartment and after dropping off my case I was then rushed back out of the apartment and into the car to be taken to the harbour where in the dark, warm evening some of the teachers had gathered after some school event. They were in a state of some refreshment and I was welcomed with open arms. It was from there that the feeding and drinking began.

I was soon to learn that this socializing, accompanied with lots of food and drink, was quite normal at school events, of which there were to be a lot over the subsequent weeks and months. Food and drink were an intrinsic part of the proceedings and there were several stages to the day. This gathering at the harbour was the last stage of this particular event with some wind down drinks, along with yet more food. Koreans will not drink without a snack of some kind, even something as simple as popcorn, but it was usually much more extravagant.

The next morning, a Saturday, I was picked up and taken to another event which was a town wide school sports day. After being introduced to the hierarchy of local education chiefs I was installed under the main gazebo and plied with food and drink for a couple of hours. Then I was dragged off to sightsee the local beach in a break in proceedings, along with a couple of drinks, before I was rushed back to the sports ground, introduced to more people with some more drinks and more food before being taken home.

I thought that was it for the day but no, an hour or two later there was a knock on the door and a teacher was there to take me to the post-sports day concert at the local civic centre. I was escorted through the theatre to the surprise and chatter of the audience, especially the giggling middle school girls that I was soon to be teaching. At the front of the auditorium I was introduced to my school principal who, as a former English teacher, seemed pleased to have the opportunity to speak to me in English. To further welcome me into the community he insisted that I go on stage and sing a song to the students. That's on stage, to sing a song to several hundred people with a couple of minutes notice.

Having just arrived, I was keen to go with the flow and not cause any problems. It is said that Koreans are the Latin Americans of Asia. Despite the Buddhist temples and adherence to Confucian doctrines with lots of bowing and deference to elders, if Koreans are crossed, upset or offended then there is no going back. They can be prone to volatile and passionate explosions of rage when offence is caused, especially the kind which involves someone losing face. Although they were very welcoming to foreigners and gave considerable leeway to newcomers whilst they adapted to their new surroundings, there was little chance of redemption if a foreigner crossed the line and caused someone to lose face, especially the school's senior staff.

From my pre-departure planning I was aware of this and so I was very reluctant to refuse the principal's request. I didn't want to upset anyone or make any enemies within my first twenty-four hours in town, but this was quite an ask. I was acutely aware that I had only just arrived and I was eager to impress, but singing on stage just wasn't one of my strong points. I also had the afternoon's booze in my system not helping me think clearly.

Amidst all this panic I had Noel Gallagher to thank because in a sudden flash, I received inspiration from Britpop and Oasis' *Wonderwall*. It was more than likely that the audience didn't know the song and so I reasoned that I could at least muddle through the first verse and chorus with no preparation, no words and no backing. I started the song off at a brisk pace and within seconds hundreds of teenage girls were clapping along. As I concluded the song after two verses and two choruses they screamed and applauded. I had passed the initiation and the principal, an important person to have on side, was delighted. Little did I know that this was the beginning of my time as a freak show cum minor celebrity in the town.

I was left alone the next day, a Sunday, to organize my meagre possessions in the apartment that was far too big for me. It wasn't until I arrived for school on the Monday that I fully realised the Korean way of drinking. I don't think there was a spare night in that first couple of weeks as I was taken from place to place and introduced to lots of people. To the principal, I was like a trophy and he could proudly say that even his school in rural Wando had a native English speaker. I was both jealously guarded and proudly shown off, especially when visitors from schools without a native English speaker were visiting.

The early Autumn was a very sociable period because the heat and high humidity of Summer had passed and the snow and bitter coldness of Winter had yet to arrive, along with the added stresses after the New Year of preparing for the end of year exams (the school year finished in February). There were staff meetings, parent teacher association meetings, English teacher meetings, science teacher meetings, almost any excuse to go to a restaurant and have a good drink. In addition, there were the big all-day school events like the picnic, the sports day and the music festival. All of these events involved a lot of drinking, sometimes even during the event.

The speed at which Koreans drink puts any talk of binge drinking to shame. The sole purpose of them drinking is to get drunk, very drunk, and very quickly. There was no going out for a quiet pint and a chat. Maybe things were a bit more cosmopolitan in the city where there were a lot more modern bars, but in Wando it was very traditional with socialising done in restaurants where meals were washed down with a lot of booze.

An evening would typically start with a brisk walk into the town as soon as the staff could leave the school which was usually around 5pm. It would be straight to the restaurant of choice which were all very similar. They were all small and sparsely decorated and the destination varied by the restaurant's individual specialty or the connection to the school (local businesses and restaurant owners who had children at the school often paid for these evenings).

Shoes off and sitting cross-legged on the floor at the low tables, the first dishes would be brought in which were usually a few snacks to help with the first round of drinking. Once we were all in, or at least the senior members of staff were, the bottles of soju, a rice-derived spirit with a strength of around 20% ABV were cracked open. The table top barbecues were warmed and the plates of raw meat were brought in for the cooking to begin.

Korean barbecue, or bulgogi, was to become a near staple diet over the next couple of years. Most restaurants in Wando specialised in only one type of meat such as pork, and then sometimes only one specialisation of pork, such as ribs or pork belly. The choice of restaurant depended on the budget with pork being the cheapest followed by chicken, which was rarely eaten, beef and then the more expensive seafood. With pork being the cheapest, I was to eat a lot of table top barbecued pork belly, 'sam-gyup-sal,' in my time there. The strips of meat were cooked on the table in front of you and then when they were ready you removed your chosen piece of meat from the grill and placed it on a large lettuce leaf. Added to it were a large piece of garlic, chili pepper and some soy bean paste. It was then wrapped into a small parcel and then eaten whole after taking a shot of the soju.

Whilst waiting for the meat to cook, the drink started to flow along with the early plates of snacks. These were often things like spicy marinated vegetables with lots of garlic, quail eggs and the ever-present kimchee which is the Korean staple dish of cold, spicy fermented Chinese cabbage, also with lots of garlic, which was eaten with every meal (and it tastes a *lot* better than it sounds).

The main drink at these gatherings was soju. It did the job quickly and was far cheaper than beer. The bottles would be already set up on the table before arriving but were not opened until the senior guest (usually the principal or deputy principal) had arrived. The first bottle would be opened and a glass of soju poured for the senior guest. He would drink it, make a noisy sound of appreciation, have a mouthful of something to eat and then offer the same glass back to whoever had offered it to him. He would then pour the recipient a drink who would down it in one, have a mouthful of something to eat and then pass the glass on. That was also the cue for the other bottles to be opened and small clusters would quickly form depending on how many people were in the restaurant and who the enthusiastic drinkers were. Soju would be speedily swilled and glasses swapped enthusiastically. It was very bad form to pour your own drink. Instead, you would wait to be offered a glass and if you were wanting one yourself, all you had to do was find a glass and offer it to someone to pour them a drink and then they would offer you one back. It was soon clear who at the table were the more willing recipients and up for a good drink.

The glass was received with two hands and a bow whilst the other person poured. There were rules to follow in how the drink was poured. Thankfully, there was some flexibility with foreigners as they learned the ropes. The main factor was age. The older you were, the more respect you were afforded and the bottle would either be poured with two hands. If one hand was used, usually by someone of similar but still younger age, the other hand touched the pouring arm at the wrist. The closer the non-pouring hand was to the wrist of the pouring hand indicated more respect being shown. For those lower down the age or job seniority scale (and back then the two were linked in the teaching profession at least) the bottle may have been poured one handed (unusual) or with the non-pouring arm touching the pouring arm at the elbow, possibly even higher or even not touching the arm but placed across the chest. When your drink was poured, there was a 'kom bae' (cheers) and down it went. It was quite complicated understanding and remembering the rules in the early days and this got harder as the quickly drunk soju soon addled the brain. It was easiest to be overly respectful and they would tell you if there was no need to be so formal. It was rude not to accept a drink, and equally rude not to offer the glass back. There would be numerous glasses moving round the table and the pace was brisk. It didn't take long to find yourself completely wasted.

As the meat was finished and you were contemplating how full you were, rice would then be brought in with a small bowl of soup followed by yet more side dishes. By this stage of the meal, the discomfort in the legs would be increasing and the inhibitions in the group decreasing. Inner thighs would be squeezed and hands held in a gesture of friendship, but it could be a little uncomfortable. Then, as soon as the food was finished, everyone would get up and we were off, though it was rarely home time. On the bigger and more boisterous nights this meant being dragged off to a 'no-rae-bang' which was a singing room. Unlike the Japanese karaoke where the singing is done in a bar performing to everyone there, in a Korean no-rae-bang the group goes into a private room which permitted much more raucous behaviour and less concern about dreadful singing performances.

If a singing room was involved in an evening's proceedings, it generally implied an elevated level of intoxication. The teachers only went to the singing room when they were wasted. Some beers would arrive and snacks to go with it, usually very rubbery dried squid or small sheets of the locally dried seaweed which were super salty and delicious. The same concept was followed with the beer as with the soju, only this time it would usually be small paper cups of beer that were passed around the group. You didn't nurse your own bottle. On some occasions, a couple of hostesses would mysteriously appear to sit with the men and pour drinks and generally smile at their small talk. Singing rooms could be excruciating if you weren't in the right frame of mind, but they were great fun when everyone was well fed and drunk enough to think that they really could sing. I didn't know any of the Korean songs that were being sung but I went along with the whole thing which was enhanced with beer and the TV screens which frequently showed a backing video of attractive women frolicking in bikinis in sun-drenched locations. I was of course asked to perform a song or two of my own choice which was much easier with a belly full of booze and having the words on screen in front. There were always some Western karaoke classics available in the song book.

Then suddenly, and without warning, time would be up and it was home time. Everyone stumbled out and made their short journey home. I would be home in bed and with the room spinning by 8.30pm. These school nights out were intense affairs with a whole evening of eating, drinking and singing compacted into just a couple of hours. Many of the restaurants and singing rooms would close quite early especially during the week because no-one seemed to go out late. You went out early; you hit the booze hard and you went home at a sensible time. In a way, it was a relief because it at least allowed plenty of time to sleep it off before heading back into school no doubt still stinking of soju and garlic.

In the first few weeks, my work schedule as well as my social schedule was hectic because every teacher commandeered me to go into their class with them, even the teachers of other subjects. This was not ideal with a hangover and was made even worse when some of the teachers who grabbed me to take me to a class then abandoned me on my own as they themselves were hungover and disappeared outside to drink coffee and smoke cigarettes.

Thankfully, this kind of thing didn't last too long once the initial novelty had worn off and I only had to endure it until lunchtime. In the afternoons, the theory was that I was supposed to hold classes with the area's English teachers to help them learn and hopefully develop their teaching. With few exceptions, most English teachers hadn't had the chance to visit or study abroad in the way UK language students would. Although their written English was generally very good and some of the handwriting from young students was immaculate, the spoken word was poor with a lot linked to confidence and the fear of getting it wrong making students reluctant to speak beyond the standard 'How are you?' 'I'm fine, thank you, and you?' which greeted me constantly all around the town.

One of the early treats was to go and visit some of the smaller schools on the outlying islands which were communities that were too small to warrant regular visits or to have their own native teacher. Some of the island teachers would come and see me for a weekly workshop but again this didn't always happen depending on their schedules. The all-important end-of-year exams took precedence over everything. Going out to the islands really did feel like stepping into another world. Wando felt small and isolated, but the island communities were even more so. They were unspoiled and peaceful and with a slow and traditional pace of life, dominated by agriculture. There were plenty of restaurants which always seemed to be well populated given that there probably wasn't that much else to do out there. The schools looked just the same as those on the mainland but they were noticeably quieter with moth-balled classrooms reflecting the population drift to the mainland over the years. The tranquillity and isolation were lovely and the schools were always grateful for visitors which would invariably mean another good lunch washed down with soju.

When attending the most isolated populated island in the district, Bogil-do, which was an hour and a half away by ferry, the school really threw a party on for us and dog was on the menu for the one and only time that I was in the country. Much as I found the idea distasteful, not wanting to cause offence I went along with it and the meat was surprisingly tasty, though I was far from comfortable with eating dog having seen some of the dog farming conditions in the hamlets around the islands. Its popularity was declining even then, and even in traditional farming areas like Wando that were keener on the idea than more progressive thinking city dwellers. People my age that I spoke to about eating dog found it as unappealing as Westerners did. It was very much something older men did, convinced as they were that it was good for keeping things working downstairs in the bedroom department.

As hectic as things were in the evenings in those first few weeks, there was also the chaos of the all-day school events to get through. The mild, sunny and dry weather allowed for outdoor events such as the annual sports day and the picnic. They were big events which took a lot of planning and organising and always ended with a 5pm dash to a restaurant, a lot of soju and a no-rae-bang. The picnic was altogether different. After walking to the picnic site which took an hour there were some organised games in the morning followed by lunch. The students were unbelievably self-disciplined and well-behaved, eating their picnics and entertaining themselves whilst the teachers got down to the serious business of lunch which was a beautiful picnic prepared by some of the mothers. Lunch also came with soju which, if it was destructive enough in the evening was even more lethal in the sunshine and fresh air. The mothers who had prepared the picnic soon started mothering me, amazed that a man was living on his own and somehow managing to look after himself and it wasn't long before a constant stream of food parcels began to arrive with box after box of delicious homemade kimchee making their way to my apartment.

Loaded with soju and a fine lunch, there would be some more activities and games in the afternoon, organised by the half-cut male teachers whilst the women teachers helped the mums clean up after the lunch. Towards the end of the afternoon, the kids would be dismissed to make their own way home whilst the teachers headed off to a restaurant for a barbecue dinner, despite being well fed at lunchtime, a lot of soju and another singing room.

By November, the easy-going part of the term was over and in December the temperature dropped and the snow arrived. The focus at the school switched to the final exams in January which would determine high school attendance for the new school year in February. All students were pushed hard, but the brightest and most talented were pushed exceptionally hard to get into the best high schools. After an intense first few months it was a very welcome break as my classes were considered superfluous compared to cramming for exams and the teachers were too stressed and overworked to be going out eating and drinking, though they would make up for it once the exams were finished.

Any shortfall in eating and drinking at my main school in Wando would be made up for on my Friday visits to a smaller school in a small village at the other end of the island. I had been going there since I arrived and it was the most beautiful journey to work. I had to get the bus and the journey took the coast road which skirted the shore front on the east side of the island.

At Gun-nae middle school I was taken under the wing of the English teacher who was the only teacher I met in my time there who saw me as a valuable resource for her and her students' learning. She was luckier than most in that her husband was a senior airline executive and the family had spent time in Canada while he did his MBA. She was thrilled to have a native English speaker to work with and she didn't abandon me to face the class alone whilst she smoked and dealt with a hangover like some of her male colleagues did. We worked the class together and then every Friday she took me across the road for lunch in one of the small local restaurants. It was so small that if there were more than a few customers you would eat your meal in the daughter's bedroom. In many small restaurants in rural towns and villages, the restaurant was at the front with the cooking and living space behind the sliding doors at the rear of the restaurant. In small rural homes, the bedding would be rolled up daily and placed in a cupboard allowing a small table to be taken in and placed on the floor and we'd sit there cross-legged enjoying our lunch surrounded by a young woman's photos and trinkets. It was bizarre.

There was no drinking at these lunches though we ate well and afterwards we would have our own workshop or discussion. I'd help her with whatever she needed whether it was her own study, helping one of the very few gifted students or preparing students for the prestigious and ultra-competitive English-speaking competitions. She would then let me sneak off early because in those first few months, Friday night was time to head off the island and up to the city of Kwangju, the provincial capital and the largest city in the south-west. There, the other foreign teachers in the programme would meet up and it was expat party time, as if there hadn't been enough partying during the week for some of us. It was a much-needed chance to relax and chat with other foreigners and compare stories.

The journey took between two and three hours depending on the route and arriving in the huge bus station on the edge of town was such a contrast to sleepy little Wando. The city was big, bright and modern but was still considered backward compared to other regions in Korea. The south-western Cholla province had an uneasy relationship with the rest of the country going back decades. It has even been argued that development of the region was deliberately held back in favour of other provinces as a punishment for its pesky democracy-aspiring politicians and protesting students during the dictatorship that lasted from the 1960s to the 1980s. With democracy established it was a bustling carefree city with teeming streets, bright lights, bustling shops and restaurants with young and not so young Koreans out enjoying themselves.

The evening would usually start with dinner and then on for drinks at whichever bar was the flavour of the moment amongst the expat community. The 'Hard Rock' was an early destination that had no connection with the American themed bars and diners of the same name. It was a blatant rip off but we weren't bothered because it was a decent bar and a good place to meet. Later, we shifted to a lounge bar that somehow skirted around late licensing restrictions by not being a bar but a shop where you chose your own beers out of the fridge and paid for them at a till but you could then sit in comfy chairs to enjoy them.

For a very different experience there were soju tents. These were temporary structures with tarpaulins over them where you squeezed in and drank soju and ate snacks. They were much cheaper drinking venues than bars but even with a rise in affluence and plenty of trendy modern bars to go to, they retained a kind of ironic appeal to the young and trendy of Kwangju that had no concept of huddling in shacks to drink as their fathers and grandfathers had no doubt done. Sundays would inevitably involve a very weary bus journey back to Wando after calling at the Shin Se Gae department store next to Kwangju bus station because it had a 'foreign food' section in the basement. Much as I loved Korean food, it was always nice to stock up on some baked beans which were impossible to find in Wando.

As the year progressed, the frequency of the school-related outings declined at the main school, thankfully, because it could get exhausting. It wasn't quite the same at Gun-nae where, as the year progressed, I didn't always head up to the city, preferring instead to spend some weekends in Wando or have friends come to visit me. On those stay at home weekends, Fridays became massive booze ups after a change of personnel at the Gun-nae school in the new academic year. Some older teachers arrived for a quiet couple of years to wind down to retirement and, away from their families who were in the cities, they were not good in their own company and enjoyed misbehaving. By being able to keep up with them in the soju and food stakes and by being a generally good sport they really took a shine to me. Learning a traditional Korean song for the no-rae-bang went down a storm and they insisted I sing it every time we were out as some of the male bonding sessions got a little out of hand.

The easy life and good food and drink seemed like too a good thing to give up and with no real idea what I was to do, I stayed on for another year. Having spent most weekends on a bus for the first year I spent more weekends locally in my second, enjoying life in Wando and with less partying at the weekends, apart from my Fridays in Gun-nae. What I couldn't have predicted when I signed my contract was the complete meltdown of the Asian tiger economies that gained momentum over the

Summer of 1997 and arrived with a bang in South Korea just as we returned to school.

The crisis deepened with each week. The salary was still being paid and the same amount went into the bank every month. Inflation wasn't an issue but those of us that were sending money home saw our salaries shrink in their sterling equivalent month after month until things stabilised the following year. There was very little going out at the school as belts were tightened and instead the soju was being drunk by foreign teachers as they shared sob stories and tried to keep each other's spirits up. Some cut their losses and went home because besides the financial implications, some people were seeing hostility from their previously friendly colleagues with some locals believing that the crisis was all the fault of foreigners. Most of us who weren't on the receiving end of xenophobia rode out the storm, steeled with soju, beer and barbecued pork belly. The slump was noticeable on the British Airways flight home that Christmas which was nearly empty. British Airways would soon stop flying to Seoul in the aftermath of the crisis and flights wouldn't be reinstated for another fifteen years.

Back at Gun-nae school on Friday afternoons, they dealt with the changing times in their own unique way by partying even harder. Sadly, at my main school in Wando there were lots of changes in the new school year and a lot of familiar faces moved on. I was left a little isolated without my regular crowd of men leading me astray, but that probably wasn't a bad thing. At Gun-nae though, many of the old faces stayed to wind down one more year to their retirement in a school that was shrinking in student numbers every year and the quiet life continued for most of them.

Island life was idyllic. The pay was good, the workload wasn't too demanding and it was a wonderful place to live and work. The feeding and drinking on Fridays continued but by the Spring of 1998 it was time to reassess things. Another contract was offered and the schools wanted me to stay, but with a heavy heart, I decided that at twenty-seven it was time to get a 'proper' job. I reluctantly said goodbye to what had been a terrific two years and headed to Seoul for the long flight home. I arrived back at Heathrow where Phil collected me.

We then went to the pub.

11 GOOD GUINNESS & BAD SOUTHERN BEER

On November 18th 2000 on a dark autumnal afternoon at Twickenham, England's Dan Luger scored a last gasp try against Australia to snatch a 22-19 victory. Just a year earlier, the Cemetery Junction housemates had watched the disappointment of the 1999 Rugby World Cup from various pubs in Twickenham and west London. Little did we know how things would change following the series of games that November. After beating the Australians, victories followed over Argentina and South Africa which would set the England team up for their steady march to world dominance over the next couple of years. In the process, they collected Six Nations titles, a Grand Slam and the small matter of a World Cup.

I had been living and working in Reading after returning from South Korea. The town centre had transformed during the two years that I was away and on my return was full of pubs and restaurants and it had also acquired a big new redevelopment in the town centre. There were some 'proper' pubs, two new Wetherspoon's and plenty of 'trendy' bars but the Monks had been left behind and had gone quickly downhill and was scruffy and unappealing. Eugene and Shirley had long gone.

Despite Reading's improved temptations, a job change made the commute unbearable and I moved down the M4 to be nearer to work. This made it even easier for us to enjoy this remarkable period in English rugby as the Cemetery Junction house-mates also drifted towards London to start their various careers. With jobs to hold down, we started getting together regularly at the weekend, and especially when there was rugby on the TV. The mid 1990s had been dominated by beer and music and the early noughties were to be dominated by beer and rugby. Saturday afternoons sitting in the pub watching the rugby became fixtures in our year and it was to be three great years of sport and beer drinking in the pub as we settled into working life.

Watching sport on television in the pub was something that we had never really done, even as students. The 1995 Rugby World Cup provided some memorable moments including Jona Lomu destroying England in the semi-final and Nelson Mandela handing over the trophy to the victorious South Africans. There had been occasional Five Nations matches as well as the odd FA cup final but we rarely went to the pub specifically to watch sport. Some of us had shared the collective trauma along with hundreds of others in the Students' Union watching *that* semi-final against Germany at Euro '96 wishing Gazza's foot had been an extra half inch longer, but they were rare occasions.

As I was settling into the suburbs, some of the others had settled into a large flat in Fulham which soon became the focus of our get-togethers. Despite its rather posh image, I was surprised just how rough and seedy parts of Fulham were. Down some of the side streets off Fulham High Road were some grotty, sparsely populated pubs that we just loved. They were dingy and the fashionable Fulham set wouldn't have touched them with a bargepole, but they were quiet, you could always get a seat, there was never a wait at the bar and the ones we chose also had large TVs or projector screens to show the rugby that we had gone there to watch.

The beer was no better in London than it was in Reading and we certainly didn't trust it in some of the pubs we went to. Fullers London Pride was the staple beer and popular as it may have been it just never did anything for me, wherever I drank it. I've even had it in the north served through a sparkler rather than flat and still it left me unimpressed. Youngs was far more palatable but we rarely seemed to find ourselves in Youngs pubs. It was still a relatively local beer with the Ram Brewery in Wandsworth a few miles away not closing until 2006. These rugby gatherings were usually on cold wintry days and with the unpredictability of the beer we quickly settled on Guinness as our London, and rugby, beer of choice. It was more expensive but it was tasty, consistent and just seemed to go so well with rugby.

This was pub pleasure at its finest. A leisurely Saturday afternoon in the pub with good friends after a long week of work. There was a common interest on those rugby days and we were all fans. Some days we sat through two or even three games, we were in no rush to go anywhere and afternoons quickly became my favourite time to be in the pub. It still is. These afternoon sessions invariably carried on into the evening either locally or maybe in central London where we quickly found a couple of favourite pubs. Things would usually be rounded off with a kebab and a night on their sofa in Fulham followed by a big fry up in a grim greasy spoon café the next morning.

We had many good times in the pub over those couple of years, but the rugby days were particularly good fun. We watched the England team get stronger and stronger to become the best team in the world and the pinnacle of this Guinness drinking in bad pubs in west London came to a head one morning in November 2003. Beer, sport and a national occasion all came together spectacularly.

For this special event, we ventured from the back-street pubs to Fulham Broadway and to the larger and brasher Bootsy Brogans where we hoped for more of an atmosphere that suited the occasion. It wasn't a day to be sat in a pub with a few smelly old men nursing their pints. This was a huge event and a climax to all the games that we had watched over the previous three years. It was to be Guinness for breakfast for us when just after 8am on 22nd November we found ourselves in the pub as England were about to take on Australia in the 2003 Rugby World Cup final. We got there in good time just after opening and got a table to ourselves, just under the screen. We settled in for what we were hoping was going to be a great morning.

The atmosphere in Bootsy Brogans was electric. The pub soon filled up with a mix of England fans as well as plenty of Aussies with everyone in a lively, if nervous mood. Whilst Australians always assume they are going to win, the English fans were the more nervous. England may have been the best team in the world, but they were playing on Aussie home soil and the Wallabies had despatched the All Blacks in the semi-final.

There was an initial shock at drinking Guinness that early in the morning, but we soon got over it and the first few pints went down without much difficulty. It was a great game and the drinking pace soon picked up as the tension rose after Australia's Lottie Tquiri won a high ball against the more vertically challenged Jason Robinson and scored the opening try. Robinson responded not long afterwards, crossing the line in a well worked move with Johnny Wilkinson and Lawrence Dallaglio. The pub erupted only for it to collectively groan a few minutes later when Ben Kay dropped the ball just as he was collapsing over the line for what would have been England's second try.

There were still plenty of nerves at half-time as glasses were refilled before a gripping second half and as the end approached, England were ahead. The half ended with some questionable scrum refereeing leading to a last gasp penalty kick from Australia which levelled the scores. We should have been celebrating. Instead, we had to refill our glasses and endure extra time.

Of course, we all know what happened next. The climax to the game was one of the great moments in televised sport. In the final moves of the second half of extra time with a rugby version of a penalty shootout looming, Matt Dawson had a cheeky run forward and gained some vital metres before Martin Johnson took the ball and ploughed into the defenders to allow the key players to get into position. The ball was recycled, thrown back to Johnny Wilkinson who did what Johnny

Wilkinson had been doing consistently for the previous three years and his drop kick sailed over the bar and between the posts to make the score 20-17 with seconds to spare. The pub erupted, but that wasn't the end. The game had to be restarted even though there were only seconds left. As soon as the clock went red Mike Catt hoofed the ball into touch for England to win the game and become the first and only northern hemisphere team to lift the Webb Ellis trophy.

It was a perfect beer and pub moment. The joy in the pub was extraordinary and the beer flowed. Three years of bachelor fun and watching almost all the games with more than a few pints of Guinness had culminated in the ultimate game and the ultimate trophy for the team that had gained momentum since 2000 and had ended up as world beaters, peaking at just the right time. By the time of the Six Nations the following Spring, the invincibility had gone and there was the first defeat at Twickenham for over three years. Clive Woodward would soon depart, bizarrely claiming that his first love was always football where he worked for a brief period before achieving success with Team GB at the 2012 games.

That was for the future though. We had another couple of pints before stumbling out into the street around midday into the bizarre mix of Fulham citizens who had no interest or awareness of the rugby and were going about their regular Saturday morning business whilst hundreds of ruddy faced rugby fans in their white shirts carried on the party, stumbling from pub to pub.

There were more drinks, some food, and some more drinks before we rounded the day off in Soho at De Hems, our favourite central London pub. It was a fitting way to end the period of London living and drinking because by the next round of internationals, we would all have dispersed.

12 REAL ALE REVOLUTION

That memorable day in Bootsy Brogans signalled the end of our own lazy Saturday afternoons in questionable pubs in west London. People were moving on with their careers and their lives and the Fulham bachelor hub was soon to break up.

I was ready for a change as well. I had been very bored and demotivated at work for some time. I was working for an airline and things hadn't been good since the momentous events a couple of years earlier when on an otherwise quiet morning, reports filtered in to the office that a plane had hit the World Trade Center in New York. There was a lot of initial uncertainty about how serious it was. It soon became clear that it was very, very serious and the office went into a flurry of activity closing flights for future bookings and working out what was where which accelerated after the US government took the unprecedented step of closing all American airspace. Some flights were turned around mid-Atlantic and some were sent to Canada.

After the event, some claimed that 9/11 was the day the Internet 'came of age,' the biggest live event that it had dealt with. They claimed that people could let others know they were safe as well as to find out what was going on at the click of a mouse. It certainly didn't seem like that in the office. It was the head office of a massive UK airline, hugely impacted by events and we had barely any idea what was going on, relying on people rushing back from 'situation' meetings to give an update before official emails could be written and circulated. The Internet had ground to a halt in the office with no pages refreshing. There were no TVs, smartphones were years away and in this supposedly amazing age of modern technology, we had to resort to huddling around an old medium wave radio that someone had found in a cupboard listening to the BBC's *Five Live* trying to find out what was going on.

When the World Trade Center towers collapsed many of us knew that things were going to be very different coming into work the following morning and a trip to the pub was essential to digest what had been a quite extraordinary day.

The airline sector was plunged into an immediate crisis and our seemingly safe jobs and promising careers were suddenly in real jeopardy. The relaxed atmosphere that had pervaded through the company before 9/11 disappeared overnight. Suddenly there was no money for anything. Stationery was rationed, staff travel cancelled in all but only the most exceptional of cases and a top down clear-out of well-paid managers began. Other airlines closed, even national carriers, and we were given daily messages of doom of gloom about how we were only days away from collapsing. The company scraped through but it was a perfect excuse for the company to slash staff numbers and cut costs in areas which were undoubtedly bloated, inefficient and superfluous and I included myself in that category. The company would function quite adequately without the graphs and spreadsheets that I produced. Change and restructuring was slow and tedious and, two years on, still hadn't been resolved and sadly I wasn't important enough to be paid off with a redundancy package. I was bored and going nowhere and, needing a change, I impulsively set a course for Yorkshire and, more specifically, the Big Six.

I quit my job and moved into a house on Ingram Street, just around the corner from the pub. From the house, it was less than a minute's walk to the pub. Fifteen years after we first settled into the snug, the Big Six was finally my local and it was to be a massive part of my life for nearly three years.

The Big Six had never left Bob, Phil and I even though the two of them had long left the town when their parents sold up and moved away in 1996. Apart from being away in Korea, I was still always drawn there when I was back in town visiting my parents which I did more regularly than when I was working compared to being a student. Knowing the Big Six was there was a big influencer in the decision to return home. It would make the transition so much easier and enjoyable and it was a done deal when the house on Ingram Street was available to rent. I wouldn't have wanted to live anywhere else in town.

When I was away working in Reading and London, any weekend back in Halifax had to involve a Friday night in the Big Six. I would just wander in and see who was there. Friday nights were always busy and a lively evening was guaranteed. The lunchtime snug crowd had gone and I'm not sure if Fred and Edgar were even still alive. Michael was very much alive but after some fallout years before he never went back. Instead he spent his time at the nearby William IV on King Cross, then still selling excellent Tetley.

The exception was Harold who still came in a few times a week. Long standing landlords Duncan and Sheila had finally retired in 1996 and the reigns were handed to a much younger man, John, who loved the pub as much as we did. He kept things just as they were and he is still there, over twenty years later. He didn't try and change anything. The tradition and smoke-stained wallpaper all stayed and he even inherited all the bric-a-brac on the shelves. He left them right where they were, including Bob's tie hanging behind the bar. Most importantly, he kept the focus on the quality of the beer. The Tetley had long gone by the time I returned permanently but there were plenty of new beers turning up on the bar from the rapidly growing number of small independent breweries that were starting up.

Bob, Phil and I had known John from our student days going in there and I had got to know him more over the years on my weekend visits. When I came home to see my parents, almost as soon as I'd dropped my bag and said hello I would head up there because Friday nights were always lively.

The other good thing about Fridays in the Big Six in the early 2000s was that you could stay late, sometimes very late. There never had been a bell in the pub. Instead the lights were flicked on and off at for last orders and for time at 11pm. After a brief break and allowing for some drinking up time, most people would drift off, but a few regulars would be allowed to stay. When everyone else had gone, the door would be locked and the bar would reopen. It would quite often be 2am when I stumbled back down across Savile Park towards home.

They were great evenings and whenever I went back which were often several months apart, I was always welcomed back as a long-lost stranger and always allowed to stay behind after hours. Harold would always forget who I was, constantly confusing me with Bob or Phil. He would then confuse them with me if they were in and I wasn't. John was a great host and would always look after me. On one evening, I was even allowed behind the hallowed bar to pull my own pint which, given how much the place meant to me, felt like a huge honour. Ridiculous I know.

After moving into Ingram Street on an April afternoon in 2004, it didn't take long to drop off my few bags and boxes and then head straight round to the Big Six for a Saturday afternoon drink in my new bona fide local. The snug where once we'd sat with Bendy Fred, Edgar and Michael was to be my new second home and it was a very different experience going there regularly rather than as a guest visitor. I knew it had always been a friendly local pub, but spending a lot of time in there I was able to realise just how friendly a community local it was. I still always preferred the left snug and although I knew some people in there, I was to get to know plenty of other people very quickly, just by sitting in the snug. People would come in, like I did, and get a pint, sit down and chat to whoever was there. People came and went, some stopping for a quick pint whilst others would settle in for the afternoon or evening. It wasn't hard to make friends in there over a couple of pints. There were no airs and graces and it was a friendly little meeting place for people to drink and chat which was such a refreshing change after living in London. Even though I had pubs even closer to my flat than the Big Six was, none of them had the warmth and certainly not the good beer of the Big Six.

When I had left Halifax in 1992, the town was still a two-beer town with Tetley and Websters owning most of the pubs. The Websters brewery closed in 1996 but by 2004 there were small independent breweries in the town and plenty of others in the surrounding area. West Yorkshire was leading the way at the time with, I believe, the most breweries in any county of England at the time. This growth of independent breweries had completely passed me by in my time overseas and then down south when we had defaulted to the same few bad pubs and Guinness to guarantee a decent drink. The choice and variety of beers on the bar was a revelation. As well as locally produced beers, there were appearances on the Big Six bar from breweries quite literally from Cornwall to Scotland.

I soon had my favourites, but my drinking habits were changed completely with the discovery of the increasingly popular golden ales. I'd never seen them before in Fullers and Youngs territory despite their history which is said to go back to 1986 when the Hopback Brewery near Salisbury began brewing a light, hoppy beer all year round. Although their legendary Summer Lightning was a bit ambitious for me as a session beer with a strength of 5% ABV, it was delicious and its appearance on the bar at the Big Six was eagerly anticipated. If you weren't in there quick, it had soon gone because once on the bar a couple of barrels would disappear in no time. It wasn't on regularly but that didn't matter because there was always a good range of beers on the bar and lots of the new breweries were adding pale beers to their portfolio that thankfully weren't as strong as Summer Lightning and were light, hoppy, 'session' beers. Early favourites came from new breweries like Newby Wyke (Grantham, established 1998), Salamander (Bradford, est. 1999) and Anglo-Dutch (Dewsbury, est. 2000).

There was constant variety on the bar at the Big Six. All the beers were kept in excellent condition and having the pub there was just too much of a temptation. I had swapped office work for self-employed outdoor work and if there was ever a time for a beer it was after a long day grafting outside in Summer weather getting sweaty and dirty. I would drop the car off and go straight round for a couple of thirst quenchers that would barely touch the sides. Although I had only rarely gone to the pub after work in London, mainly due to not really liking any of the pubs, I quickly became a huge fan of the tea time drink with 5pm becoming my own cocktail hour. There was always a lively tea time crowd in the Big Six, even on traditionally quiet days of the week.

It had always been a real community pub and back in the late 1980s when we first started venturing in, the old ladies who lived on the street would come in to the pub in their slippers to buy a bottle of brown ale or stout to take back home whilst they were watching Coronation Street. They would then wander back in later to return the bottle. It was used as an extension of people's houses, a place to call for a pint whilst waiting for your tea to cook or to buy a pint and take it home. Things hadn't changed over the fifteen years since I was last regularly going in. The community had changed over the years and a lot of the older folk that were in their slippers in the late 1980s were no longer around. A lot of younger people had bought or were renting the small houses in the street and a lot of them used the pub.

All of us living on Ingram Street were regulars in there and the snug became a friendly place to go and spend some time. There would always be someone in to chat to and there was always a warm welcome whether you went in every day or once or month. For a single bloke who enjoyed a beer, there was no better place. It was, and remains, the best pub in the world. Long may it stay that way.

13 WORKING IN PUBS 3

I had a lot of fun pulling pints at the Portman and the Monks' Retreat between 1991 and 1996. They were two very different pubs but both were great experiences with some good people. I enjoyed it and was good at it but I viewed it very much as a student thing, a financial necessity to avoid getting completely bogged down in student debt. When I left, I wanted to put pint-pulling behind me and I vowed to never pull one again. For ten years, I stuck to my word.

After some difficult circumstances, I found myself back behind the bar and in a very different pub to what I'd known at the Portman and the Monks. I was needing work and a Big Six friend was the bar manager at a new pub in nearby Sowerby Bridge who said to pop down if I was interested in a few hours. I went down and was very impressed with the pub. Little did I know at the time just how much Sowerby Bridge was changing. The pub where I was about to start work was one of those driving this change and was called The Works, just off the main street through Sowerby Bridge. It was to be an interesting, and very different, third chapter of pub working. The Portman of the early 1990s was the old-fashioned pre-Beer Orders tied-house model that had served the industry, rightly or wrongly, for decades. Brewery-owned pubs sold their own products with a manager living 'above the shop.' The Monks was very different again because it was a large corporate chain, but was merely a retailer. It had no connection with breweries and was able to pick and choose what products it sold, very much like the 'free houses' of old, but on a huge scale. Managers were held accountable for sales and rewarded well for success and moved along if not making the grade. There was none of the warmth of traditional pubs and I have never been in one that has felt even remotely like a traditional 'local' pub.

The Works was a different model again. It was a very ambitious start up project in what was once a small factory. It was an independent with no connection to any brewery and so, like Wetherspoon's, it could pick and choose which products it wanted to sell. It was a large venue, with plenty of standing space in front of the bar and plenty of tables and chairs for food. Despite the size, it aspired to create a 'traditional' local pub feel, run with a personal touch. Its décor was a modern take on a traditional theme, so there was lots of exposed brickwork, wooden flooring, salvaged furniture and church pews and antique bric-a-brac. It offered traditional events like quiz nights and it wanted to put itself out there as being part of the community and involved with community activities.

The centre of the offering was the real ale. That was the focus and the selling point of the pub, although Carling, Kronenbourg 1664, Guinness and a draught cider were also available. There were three permanent beers on the bar from the long established and award-winning Timothy Taylor brewery in nearby Keighley. There was the session strength Golden Best as well as the slightly stronger Best Bitter joining the well-known Landlord. Alongside the three Taylor beers there were also five pumps for guest ales with an additional three spare pumps if needed. The aim of the beer portfolio was to offer a weaker session beer (under 4% ABV), one normal strength beer (between 4% and 5% ABV), a strong beer, a dark beer or mild and one other.

It was a large building, both in terms of floor space as well as height. The main bar area was an expansive two storey high open room. There was a large log burning stove but even with that it took a while to get the place warmed up. My opening shift was the awful 3pm until closing on Sundays. The pub was a busy place on Sundays with a relentless trade of over-lapping drinkers from the lunchtime only drinkers, followed by the afternoon session, followed by those that came out at tea time and then the night time crowd. Some of them were out for the whole duration.

It was a full on solid six hours of hard graft that always seemed so much longer. It really felt like it was a shift twice as long. It did start to ease off around 9pm when people remembered that they had work in the morning, but any lull in the serving was spent catching up with all the other duties that had been neglected in the rush. It was never really packed at the bar with people jostling for attention, but it was relentless all day.

These busy Sundays lasted until the decision was taken to have music in the afternoon. By music, it was an old bloke and a keyboard. He was a lovely chap and he came into the pub regularly. He was an amateur keyboard player, very enthusiastic and offered to play for free, I guess as much as a hobby or an excuse to get out of the house. He just enjoyed tinkling away. The boss, who was frequently well lubricated by mid-afternoon on a Sunday after a phase of hosting informal Sunday lunches in the flat upstairs, thought it was a wonderful idea. Unfortunately, it was excruciating to listen to. It just didn't work. He was a competent player, certainly not amazing, and he was not the greatest vocalist, but he played cheesy keyboard tunes and it was very *Phoenix Nights*. People voted with their feet over the weeks saying that they'd stay for a couple more if it wasn't for the 'turn.' I fed back what customers were saying, but it wasn't my decision and the piano man stayed. Having fewer customers in did make the shift a bit more bearable though.

It didn't take long before I was hoovering lots of spare shifts at The Works. Added to that I was picking up work in other pubs on the Sowerby Bridge circuit. There was a good camaraderie between many of the pubs in the town. Some people were working for themselves, some were in a pubco-owned pub and some were brewery installed managers. Each had different commercial considerations and everyone's pub was different. There wasn't a feeling of competition, but of mutual support because the same customers moved around each other's pubs and a healthy pub offering in the town was good for drawing more people in to everyone's benefit. Whatever the differences were in pub aesthetics, customer base and ownership, the common theme amongst them all was that they served terrific beer.

The extra work started with the Puzzle Hall, a pub that I hadn't been to since 1988 when Bob and I visited it just the once to drink Wards beer. A much loved and respected local character and beer fan called Mick Stokes had produced the weekly *Pubpaper*. This was an A4 sized fanzine type publication which was about 20 pages thick and contained bits of news and jokes. The largest section was in the middle which had the beer listings of pubs over the coming week. Pubs paid a small fee to promote their pub by listing their beers. Beer fans really did pay attention to what beers were going to be available at certain pubs. Copies of the magazine were sold to the pubs and they were left as communal reading material and it was a very popular read amongst drinkers.

Sadly, Mick died suddenly at home one night not long after I had started at The Works. He was particularly well known in Sowerby Bridge. He occasionally came into The Works and he was a long-standing regular at the Puzzle Hall. The pub community rallied round and staff and customers were going to attend his funeral en masse. Before heading to the crematorium, some of the mourners organized a pub crawl from the Big Six to the Puzzle Hall which involved a bus load of drinkers. I was asked to help out given that I was available and Puzzle staff plus myself met at The George, just below King Cross, which was to be their second call. We were ready in numbers behind the small bar to serve them as quickly as possible when they arrived given that there were going to be around forty people turning up all at once and on a tight deadline. Once they were supplied, we jumped into the car and headed to the Shepherd's Rest further down the hill to repeat the process there before heading to the Puzzle where they had time for a longer drink or two before going on to the funeral.

Not knowing him and not planning to go to the funeral, I was asked to 'keep an eye' on the Puzzle whilst they were away and to be ready for when people started drifting back. Nigel, a lovely bloke who was running the Puzzle at the time, was still a near stranger and he was leaving me in charge of his pub, and an iconic one at that, for a couple of hours. It took a while to get cleaned up and get everything ready for their return and then I could sit down with a pint, master of my domain. No passing customers came in and so there wasn't much else to do whilst waiting in a deserted pub, except to check out the beer. It was a terrible hardship.

People eventually started drifting back from the funeral and I stayed to help for another couple of hours. Before leaving I was then poached by the Puzzle to do some extra hours there which was followed not long after by offers from the Shepherd's Rest and The George. There seemed to be as many hours as I wanted and it quickly got to the point where, especially at the weekend, I was working at three different pubs in a day, starting at The George, then speed walking down the hill to the Shepherd's Rest and then on to either The Works or the Puzzle. It was nice to be in demand, but it was tiring work for a minimum age reward.

The Works had only been open for a few months when I started working there and it was very much an ongoing project. Although the bar area was completed, there were still plenty of other projects on the go which were frustratingly delayed by the quality and speed of some of the work being done with friends and acquaintances often being employed as part of the 'community spirit,' rather than expert tradesmen who might have cost more but would have got the job done quicker and with better results.

It was an ambitious project for an experienced pub operator, never mind a sole trader trying to develop a project with the perils of long hours and generating sufficient cash flow. The owner had spent plenty of time in pubs, but had no experience in running them and with trying to get the business up and running as well as the ongoing building work, things were chaotic at first. Some of the staff were running riot when not supervised, much as I had done fifteen years earlier admittedly, but it seemed so *wrong* when they were doing it. We got away with it at the Portman because we tried to be reasonably discreet, but too many people there got away with murder because they were the favourites and could do no wrong. She only saw what she wanted to see and there was always one rule for one and one for another. The same went for customers as well. The 'rules' changed constantly depending on mood, alcohol and who the person was. She wanted high standards but was very inconsistent in the mixed messages she gave as to how they were applied. I knuckled down and got on with it, but it was very interesting watching things with the benefit of age and experience.

It was successful though, or at least it seemed to be because it was a busy place. Whilst not to everyone's taste, it was a bold ambition and it was different to most of the other pubs in Sowerby Bridge. There was good footfall and although lunchtimes were generally quiet, at least until the kitchen finally opened, the afternoons picked up and there was a very good tea time trade, especially on Fridays. Weekend evenings were extremely busy, but that was what I had known at the Portman and the Monks. A lot of customers were Sowerby Bridge based but the pub did draw people in from much further afield. Sowerby Bridge began to get more popular as its reputation for decent pubs grew.

The pub had its merits and as someone who likes daytime drinking, I could see the appeal. It was light, airy and quiet and a nice environment to enjoy some top-quality beer. At the weekends, I just couldn't see the appeal at all. It was maybe a sign of age, but although it wasn't as hectic as the Monks, it was still packed, especially between 8.30 and 10pm. People congregated in the area between the bar and the door, it was a jostle to get to the bar and no matter how hard we worked, people were frequently left waiting for quite some time to get their drink with the bar two or three deep, like a town centre Wetherspoon's but with better and more expensive beer. It wasn't what The Works was supposed to be all about to me when it was so busy, loud and smoky. We struggled to sell the drinks and keep the standards we would have liked. I much preferred the 'other' Works, the one that existed for about seventy-four of the eighty-two hours a week it was open where there was a nice ambience, chatty bar staff and time for customers to contemplate and seek advice about what beer they would like. On Friday and Saturday nights people flooded in and we tried to sell them beer as fast as we could. The glass washing machine and the ice machine were hopelessly ill-equipped to cope because they were designed for much lower-volume pubs and it got quite stressful, but it was work and there was plenty of it.

The Puzzle Hall was very different and I did occasional weekend stints there as well as a regular Monday night slot. The area behind the bar was tiny and that always made for good fun in the confined space when it got busy, all very tactile and flirty. The Puzzle had retained a loyal and regular following over the years, especially from those with more 'alternative' lifestyles and interests such as musicians, artists and narrowboat residents. It also served quality cask ale and it was regularly listed in CAMRA's Good Beer Guide. It was a bit scruffy and a bit dark, but that was all part of the charm. It was a friendly place and popular amongst the local music scene where bands played regularly. The pub was small and it didn't take much for the place to be full and raucous, especially when there was a band playing.

For a pleasant change, the Shepherd's Rest Saturday night shift where I was a regular for a while was a breeze. It was such a contrast to the bedlam of The Works where I worked on Friday nights. It was quiet enough to only need myself behind the bar and, ironically, the quietest pub I had worked in had by far the biggest bar area. There was acres of space to move around in compared to falling over each other as had been the case in so many other places that I had worked. It was a nice quiet community local serving mainly those that lived in the terraced houses behind the pub. Sasha, the boss, was a lovely and very switched on young woman running it for the Ossett Brewery and had worked hard to take on what had been a difficult pub and transform it.

The crowning glory to this third stage of my pub career was being asked not only to work at the Big Six but to run it for one weekend whilst John was away. I was thrilled. The Big Six, somewhere that had been so important to me over the years, was going to be 'mine' for the weekend. I was really looking forward to it and with minimal instructions and a total desire not to completely screw it up, I nervously opened the doors at 3pm on the Friday with a long, long weekend ahead of me.

I was solo for the first stage of the Friday afternoon because the pub opened early especially for a regular crowd that came over from a nearby school. The small group of teachers soon expanded into the tea time crowd when the pub started to fill with its regular crowd coming in for a much-needed beer after a week of work. From there, it never stopped. The notorious Big Six Friday nights continued as they always had and it was soon a full house. The regular Friday staff were behind the bar and knew what they were doing and didn't need or want me interfering so that left me to chat, drink, collect glasses, supervise and change the occasional barrel. It was great.

After what was a very busy night and a ten hour stretch for me, there was then the 'afters.' It was almost expected from the regulars that I would keep the place open, being well known as partial to a late drink myself in the past. I was having a great time and, although I was tired, with a few pints inside me it didn't take much to agree. The regular staff knocked off at their usual time and I was on bar duty. I thought about an hour would be sufficient for people to have an extra drink or two. Of course, that didn't happen and it was around 3am that the last customers left. That gave me a quick turnaround to get some sleep and have everything ready for opening again at noon on Saturday for another twelve hours.

It was exhausting but I was really enjoying it. I'd enjoyed the sense of responsibility at the Puzzle after Mick's funeral and that was only for a few hours in a pub which I liked but still barely knew. The expected slightly quieter night on the Saturday didn't happen and it was surprisingly busy, almost as busy as the Friday. It was nice sunny weather and the football World Cup was on which may have contributed to people going out, but at last orders I was dead on my feet. I had to limit the after-hours drinks to an hour after closing, much to the disappointment of those that wanted to stay longer.

I was there to supervise and manage rather than being behind the bar, but the control freak in me, as well as not wanting anything to go wrong on my watch, meant that I was a constant presence all weekend. Sunday was quieter and I could take it a little bit easier with a bit of time off in the afternoon before returning in the late afternoon and a Sunday night that was considerably less hectic than the previous two nights. I handed the keys back to John on his return on the Monday after a busy but incident free weekend. It had been such a privilege to oversee the one pub that had been so important to me over the years. Phil was extremely jealous.

Then back at The Works, something happened which took me completely by surprise. The bar manager was leaving and the owner promptly offered me her role. Regardless of the many issues that we had over time, I will always be grateful to her for giving me the opportunity and a full-time job when I desperately needed one. Dashing around different pubs for minimum wage work was fine but, aged thirty-five, a regular job with regular hours was infinitely preferable even if it did commit me to one pub rather than having the variety that I had.

Although most of the hours were still behind the bar, it was a supervisory role with responsibility for stocks, cash, the rota and, most importantly, the beer. My cellar management knowledge and skills really stepped up a gear and I learned so much about running a real ale cellar. For all the pints I had pulled at the Portman and the Monks, I was never involved in what went on behind the scenes in running a pub. I don't even recall going into the cellar at the Portman because a cellar-man was employed for that very purpose.

There is a skill in running and managing a cask ale cellar. Good beer doesn't just happen. Not doing the basics right will make all the difference between a good and a bad pint. Perfectly good beer delivered by the brewery can be easily ruined once it gets into the cellar if it isn't looked after properly. It is astonishing that still in pubs bar staff will say that they have a new barrel coming on shortly; 'Yeah, it's fresh; it was delivered this morning.' Carling can be delivered and served the same day, but cask ale can't. Cask ale is a living, organic product and it must be looked after and served properly. It needs to be stored correctly and at the right temperature, left to settle, prepared for serving with the 'tap and vent' and then served through clean lines. The lines at the works were cleaned every Thursday morning. I used to go down at 9am specifically to do it. One of us would do the cask lines and one the keg lines and we would be rushing to finish in time to open at 12. It's a time-consuming job but worth it.

The racking, venting and tapping of barrels is a skill I was taught and I got obsessive about. I would spend a lot of time choosing and getting the beers lined up in succession, looking at variety as well as expiry dates and chalking up the planned sequence up on the blackboard. I enjoyed learning about the vagaries of different beers. The Timothy Taylor Landlord required special attention because of its volatility and it required careful tapping and lengthy venting for it to be right, whereas a mild could be vented, tapped and served much quicker.

Barrels are put on to the rack and wedged in place to minimize the chance of disturbance. The sediment that is inherent in cask ales needs time to settle and the barrels must be left alone. Once there had been enough settling time and it was getting nearer sale, the next action, venting, required tapping a small peg into the hole at the top of the barrel. This allowed air into the barrel and for it to breathe. Once that had been done, the shelf-life of the beer began ticking. The venting peg was porous and so allowed air in and out but in a more restricted capacity. A solid peg could then be added after it had vented to stop air going in and out and to keep the barrel fresher for longer.

Tapping required driving a plastic tap into the barrel, to which the serving pipes would be attached. If the tap was hit too hard the barrel could be disturbed and more time would be needed to allow the contents to settle again. If it wasn't hard enough the seal wouldn't be secure and there would be beer all over the cellar floor. It was important to have the barrels all set up and tapped and ready to go so that the serving pipes could simply be attached with minimal disturbance to the barrels. I really enjoyed getting the cellar set up and keeping it clean, tidy and organised and this was made so much easier because the cellar was massive with lots of room to move around.

It was hard work, long hours and at times deeply frustrating but I did feel honoured to be part of such a flagship project. The problem was, I wasn't sure if it was work that I wanted to be doing forever and if I did, I certainly didn't want to be doing it for someone else. There was an awful lot going on behind the scenes in the final few months and it was a challenging time for a lot of people. It was time to move on and, tempting as it was to stay in the trade, I decided against it. I wasn't going to be pulling any more pints. But I had said that before hadn't I?

14 WORKING IN PUBS - 4

So far, nearly ten years later, I haven't pulled another pint. I have been more than happy to have had my pub experience in front of the bar instead of behind it. The Works ended a pub career that had, with interruptions, lasted sixteen years and had been an invaluable experience in how pubs work and how the people that work in them and drink in them operate. As my interest in the beer world got deeper and wider as I got older, that experience allowed some real perspective when reading the blogs, comments and tweets of people who are quick to criticize but clearly have never worked in a pub.

Sadly, bar staff are seen too often as second-rate citizens and the pub trade is one that too many people look down on. True, some bar staff are useless, but there are plenty that aren't. There are plenty that work hard, actually like people and are really keen on trying to deliver a good service rather than grunting and slouching.

Working in pubs is always interesting, usually fun and provides a real insight into human nature. The pubs I worked in and the people I worked with were all different. The one constant was that they were all wonderful places to work (at least, most of the time). If you have the right temperament, attitude and personality then pubs can be wonderful places to work, especially if you find a pub that suits you and you have decent, like-minded people around you. I was always lucky on both counts. I liked all the pubs I worked in and the people I worked with.

On a personal level, working in a pub can do wonders for an individual's inter-personal skills and self-confidence. I would recommend it for any young person's CV because it is also a great way to learn about team-working, customer service and taking responsibility. You can be thrown together with a bunch of very diverse people working in hot, confined and at times stressful conditions and you can either learn, adapt and make a success of it or crack under the strain. Plenty of people did over the years. If you're not up to the job, or you don't enjoy it, it is apparent and very off-putting for a customer.

Working in a pub can develop your social skills, especially if someone is a bit shy or lacking in confidence. There is no hiding behind a bar. You have to face the public and interact with all kinds of people. You can meet plenty of interesting people in pubs, both in front of and behind the bar, as well as more than the occasional bore. In the right place and with the right people it can be so sociable that it can seem like you're getting paid to go out. A lot of my wages at the Portman and the Monks especially were handed back over the bar as we partied with each other when we weren't working because we all got on so well.

However, for all the benefits, bar work can be extremely demanding. Working in pubs that have a busy weekend trade, like all the main places that I have worked, can be hot, sweaty, achy and physically exhausting. Doing twelve hours or sometimes more on a weekend shift in a place like the Monks or The Works can leave your legs aching for two days.

You can also learn a lot about other people by spending time working in pubs. All the pubs that I have worked in attracted a wide range of customers. I've never been interested in trendy or 'niche' pubs. I've always worked in pubs where everyone is welcome whether you are in a suit or in overalls. Beer is a great leveller and 'public houses' should be places where everyone is equal and can rub shoulders with each other. Part of your presence behind the bar should be to facilitate that, when you have chance at least, by chatting to customers and making them feel welcome, though that is something that is far easier to do on Tuesday nights rather than on Fridays.

I don't think for one minute that I was the world's greatest bar man but I was pretty good, even if I do say so myself. I worked hard and diligently and paid attention to detail. I could also pull a consistently good pint which was something I took a lot of pride in doing with every one because I have high expectations when I am the customer.

I had the right attitude and I worked damned hard, perfecting techniques at the Monks especially to serve multiple customers at once and was more than able to move up through the gears when it was necessary as it got busier and busier. I would do back to back twelve hour shifts if they were available and keep on top of all the peripheral but important things like clearing tables promptly, resetting furniture after people left, emptying ash trays and so on. These are all the little things that people don't often notice when they are done, but leave a bad impression on customers when they aren't. I hate walking into a pub and for there to be dirty glasses, empty crisp packets and spilt beer on the tables, and especially so when the bar staff are stood leaning against the back of the bar with their arms folded looking bored or chatting to each other. There should always be something to do when working in a pub, even a quiet one. There's always something to tidy, wipe or clean and, if absolutely everything is done, then that is time to talk to the customers at the bar. It's what a lot of people that stand or sit at the bar want, especially those drinking on their own. They want a bit of interaction.

Keeping a positive attitude is important but it can be difficult at 10pm on a Saturday night after a fifty or sixty-hour week. Whilst some bar staff are just terrible at any time with a complete lack of oomph, some might not be quite as perky as you expect because they are absolutely knackered. A lot of young people working in pubs have often done a day job as well, like I did in the early days, and it can be hard to keep that smile on your face when you are dead on your feet.

Customers can have high expectations and rightly so, but they can also be very unpleasant. Sadly, too many people are utterly foul to those working in pubs, having some perceived sense of superiority over those who are merely serving them drinks. Attitudes towards the service sector and the people that work in it are messed up in the UK. Similarly, the attitude in too many parts of the service sector doesn't help address the situation with poor training, poor wages and poor career structures with bar work often seen as the kind of work you do because you can't get any other. Many years working and living abroad have made me realise just how bad service can be in the UK, but sweeping generalisations are unfair and there are plenty of exceptionally run places. As going to the pub becomes ever more expensive (and, sadly, rarer) I for one choose selectively. New places are tried as well as old favourites, but bad experiences are not repeated. Thankfully, there are places that really are putting service at the heart of what they do, and the small, new independent outfits seem to be doing things so much better.

Customers are customers though, and without them, pubs wouldn't be in business. One of the downsides about working in a pub is that it can make you realise just how *awful* the general public can be. The Monks was by far the worst and Portman the best and there were some deeply unpleasant individuals in The Works. I'm not sure if it means we have got progressively ruder as a society, that southerners are ruder than Yorkshire folk (though I'm sure that's true) or that I just notice it more and am less tolerant as I get older. The Monks did seem to attract some loutish behaviour (my third punch in the face was there on an admittedly quiet Wednesday night of all times). We did have bouncers at one point but that was at the council's insistence for all town centre pubs. They were a tremendous help because they were always more than willing to bundle out a gobby student or a football fan that had had too much Fosters Ice.

There were no bouncers at The Works, and it didn't need them. There wasn't trouble as such, but customers were frequently very rude. One way that The Works made sure 'certain' customers were actively discouraged from coming in was through the products that were sold. As a free house, it was free to sell any product from any supplier. The focus of the offering was real ale and the appeal was to a wide demographic, not just young kids out on the weekend. Lager, regular spirits and a selection of good wine was sold, but although the boss thought herself a great lefty-liberal champion of the people of every background and persuasion, free of pretentiousness and snobbery, she didn't stock drinks like Bacardi Breezers or WKD, 'mainstream' brands of bottled beer or some shots because she didn't want 'those kind of people' in the pub. There were plenty of other places in Sowerby Bridge to cater for them. It does sound elitist and snobbish given that I think a pub should be a 'public house' available to all, but in the harsh reality of running a pub, there are some customers that you just do not want.

With customers, manners cost nothing. Even on the busiest of evenings every customer got a 'Yes please?', a '£x.xx please' and a 'Thank you.' Every customer, without fail. They might not have got the dazzling conversation or hilarious banter that they had on a quiet afternoon, but they always got an acknowledgement and thanks for their custom. It was frequently not reciprocated.

Rudeness from customers came in so many forms. Perhaps the most irritating were the basics, the lack of 'please' and 'thank you.' The young were far, far worse. There were plenty of young lads that would come to the bar and just shout 'three pints of lager' (it was always lager drinkers, *always*). They would be met with a 'pardon?' The request would be repeated, and responded to with another 'pardon?' The round would then be repeated for a third time. If they hadn't got what I was looking for then I would have no problem saying something along the lines of 'Sorry, I thought you said please, but I must have misheard you.' It usually left them gob-smacked and even embarrassed if they were thinking they were being a bit macho in front of a woman. It might have been petty on my part but it was basic manners and people seem to think they can forget about being decent when the person they are in a pub buying a drink.

Equally rude was the Reading trend of throwing banknotes on to the bar after ordering, something I had never seen at the Portman though it was behaviour that was creeping in at The Works. It was not uncommon for drinks to be ordered - with a please and a thank you admittedly - and the note would then be tossed onto the bar whilst the conversation with their mate continued. Even if they hadn't had chance to throw the note on the bar, if you asked for the money and held your hand out, they would still throw the note down. So of course, there was only one course of action and that was to throw their change on to the bar. Well, not quite throw, but to put it on the bar, even if they held their hand out for it. And because there were no beer towels or beer mats at Wetherspoon's, there was often quite a bit of liquid on the bar so they got their change wet.

Of far more annoyance at the Monks, and again something I had never experienced in Yorkshire although, again, it was creeping in at The Works was the tendency for blokes waiting at a busy bar to lean over as far as possible waving their banknotes and yelling 'when you're ready mate!' This even happened on quiet days in Reading and even in some cases when approaching the bar and the bar was quiet. If you were in the middle of serving someone, they would announce their presence with a 'when you're ready mate.' It really used to grate.

Nobody likes waiting at the bar to get served but, generally, decent bar staff will *try* and mentally note who is next and serve in turn. It is more difficult the busier the place is, but you always tried. The intention is there to try and serve in turn and getting served is not determined by who shouts loudest. No matter how hard you try when working, in busy bars sometimes people do get overlooked and get served out of turn. It's frustrating as a customer, I know it is, but sometimes it just happens. It isn't *usually* deliberate or laziness on the part of the staff. Someone maybe caught their eye or maybe they just genuinely haven't noticed that someone has sneaked in there after you. One thing was certain though. The louder and ruder that customers were, the longer they waited because they would be deliberately knocked back one place in the mental queue.

Christmas brought out the worst in customers. If you were a barman needing money there were always lots of extra shifts available, but apart from the Portman it was always a horrible time to be working in a pub. The Portman was great because we were up to our regular tricks of drinking our way through each shift. Plus, even though it was busy it was rarely the three deep at the bar kind of busy that other places were. The one Christmas that I was there for the full Christmas and New Year period, 1991, we had a huge stein glass clearly marked with 'Christmas Tips' behind the bar. People were very generous with leaving little bits of change for our Christmas party that we were going to have in the New Year. For customers that were rude and who paid with a note, 50p would be taken from the change. If you were exceptionally rude then £1 would be taken. Most people never checked their change and if they did, you just played dumb, apologised and gave them the pound back but this rarely happened. We had a momentous day out in Leeds with the proceeds of that stein and a significant chunk of it came from rude customers.

The Monks and The Works were far worse because they were both popular places for work Christmas parties and nights out. I hate work Christmas parties. They can be guaranteed to bring out the worst in people. Plenty of people go to the pub with their work colleagues for a quick pint after work or have regular Friday drinks. Then along comes Christmas, the one time of the year when people who never go to the pub go to the pub. It's the time of year when people get too drunk, often at someone else's expense, and start telling people what they really think of each other, god or bad, resulting in booze-fuelled arguments and tears or even a shag in a Wetherspoon's toilet cubicle. It can bring out the truly horrible parts of people's personalities. There's often a boss on one of these nights, holding court at the bar with a circle of staff around him whilst he shouts louder and louder and expects to be served as soon as he is ready regardless of how busy the pub is, usually by leaning over the bar waving a note in the air shouting 'when you're ready mate!' When you get to him, he has no idea what his group wants to drink and he has to go around everyone individually with usually everyone having a different drink and always, *always*, the cliché of clichés in every blog post on the subject, someone orders a Guinness at the end. It takes so much longer to serve them this way yet they are the first to complain if they themselves are waiting.

By far the worst Christmas was 2005 when I was briefly stranded in London between jobs and I was temporarily working at a party venue in the City of London. These were huge corporate events and I cycled from Paddington into the City to do increasingly longer shifts because my experience, graft and use of English as a first language gave me an advantage over the European students working there. The huge marquees accommodated different functions each evening from standard Christmas parties to extravagant corporate events.

Regardless of how expensive the occasion or how professional the attendees, the behaviour and outcome was still pretty much the same. Generally, bottled beer and wine by the glass was included in the guests' admission with spirits available as paid-for items. It started off well with a very well-behaved celebrity function which was a Jamie Oliver Foundation fund-raiser hosted by the surprisingly tall Jamie Oliver with music by the unbelievably small Jamie Cullem. Also performing was the very pretty Joss Stone who I almost knocked clean over as she came bounding through the dining area singing on a cordless microphone. Thankfully I avoided a potentially hugely embarrassing collision and scuttled off back to the bar where I earwigged on a conversation between Cat Deeley, Paddy O'Brien and Dermot O'Leary.

This pleasant evening serving well-behaved celebrities bidding more on charity auctions than I have ever earned in a year was followed by the deep dark depths of the Christmas party season. I enjoy a free bar as much as anyone and some of the nights were a totally free bar, including spirits, with people wanting 'quadruple vodka and cokes, when you're ready mate' - and without the 'please' obviously. Although I wasn't standing any nonsense, the way people, both men and women, spoke to the Spanish and Italian girls working there was disgraceful. Maybe they do work hard all year for their company, maybe they felt like they were entitled to a reward but the appalling binging on spirits and the loathsome behaviour it produced made me want to rip their throats out.

Then, no sooner is Christmas over and it is New Year's Eve, the most over-rated night of the year. Working in a pub has its advantages. You're getting paid to avoid being in the crush on the other side of the bar and in a pub like the Portman you could still get plastered whilst working, as we did. Then there was usually a staff party which went on for a few hours by which time, as most nightclubs kicked out at 2am in Halifax and Reading, the crowds had dispersed and taxis became available again.

In Reading I was surprised at the number of people that came in to the pub asking for tickets for New Year's Eve. Tickets? For a pub? It seemed to be standard practice at the time down south which was no doubt a nice little earner at £10 cash for an entry ticket that didn't go through the till or the books. The Monks didn't do tickets and it was just another evening, but Eugene controlled the numbers much more so than normal so the pub didn't get too overcrowded and it was a steady evening working, easier than some Saturday nights and certainly a welcome change from the pre-Christmas rush. Eugene did sneak a few trusted lieutenants across the road to the Old Society for a couple of pints in our break on the inevitable student holiday double shift before the enforced jollity of the evening began and he turned a blind eye to a few swift halves if we were discreet. We had a good staff party, but I never enjoyed New Year's Eve. I'd rather be in bed. Roll on January when everything goes back to normal.

15 A LOVE LOST AND NEW LOVES FOUND

Enjoyable as it was, I wasn't ready to commit to a career in the pub trade and I successfully retrained and switched career to a profession that I am still in ten years later.

This career move also coincided with the end of my carefree bachelor days. Visits to the Big Six snug sadly became fewer and further between and the house by the Big Six was traded for a move to the other side of town in Hipperholme which was originally a small settlement separated from Halifax by Beacon Hill. It still retains its own identity and has a nice feel to the place. On much higher ground and away from the early power sources, it was never really industrialised like other parts of the town, although there was a lot of quarrying at one point including Brookes who had patented the non-slip paving slab at the end of the nineteenth century, but the quarry had closed in 1969.

It's a very pleasant bit of suburbia and there were a few pubs to explore, especially given that it was a part of town that I wasn't familiar with. The popular Whitehall on the busy crossroads was lively and it did do a good pint of what was becoming one of my favourite pale beers, Golden Pippin from the increasingly popular Copper Dragon brewery in Skipton (though the brewery has had some recent difficulty after rapid expansion). The Hare and Hounds had bad beer, good Guinness, no atmosphere, a very welcoming landlord and lots of potential (which has been realized recently with its transformation into an acclaimed food pub) whereas the Country House was just awful before it was completely transformed into the impressive Tannery.

I had heard of a pub called the Travellers somewhere in Hipperholme that was supposed to be a good pub. When we eventually found it, hidden away down the Halifax Old Road, it was wonderful. It was a proper community pub, very similar in ambience to the Big Six, and by then it was owned by the expanding Ossett Brewery, owners of the Shepherd's Rest where I had worked briefly and the terrific Three Pigeons just outside Halifax town centre. It had been sympathetically restored with stone flags, re-upholstered furniture and a fresh coat of paint. It allowed dogs and had an impressive range of Ossett Brewery beers as well as five rotating guest beers. This was becoming the norm for these revitalised real ale pubs. Two or three beers wasn't enough. There had to be a six-plus range and a variety of styles in the offering. Plus, being a brewery owned pub, they could sell their own beers cheaper than guest beers and at the time the basic session beer Pale Gold was under £2 per pint. It was a proper pub, well run, clean, nice to go in and open to all. There was a loyal crowd of regular tea time drinkers who you could always strike up a chat with. It was popular because it was a nice, traditional pub with good beer served by pleasant staff and it ticked all the boxes. The only drawback was the steep walk back up Tanhouse Hill to go home.

Slightly less of a climb was a new place that opened in Hipperholme not long after moving there. Dave Earnshaw began brewing beer in the early 2000s and I had first met his beers and especially the lovely Jamaican Ginger when working at the Puzzle Hall Inn in Sowerby Bridge where the manager had been an early champion of the brewery, unlike some other real ale pub proprietors in the town. His beer was never sold in The Works.

Having outgrown his initial premises, the brewery moved to a site in Hipperholme in the shadow of one of the red bricked buildings from the former Brookes quarry and he set about establishing his brewery there. The brewery was housed in what were surplus portacabins from the Channel Tunnel build and the brewing vessels were from a defunct Firkin pub. The Halifax Steam Brewery had a home.

The portacabins were put together and the 'building' was in two halves. The brewing side was a hive of activity whereas the other half sat empty. It had an art Deco themed bar, tables and chairs but no permission to open what Dave wanted, a brewery tap in which customers could drink his beers which were brewed on site. The trouble was that the good citizens of Hipperholme were not happy with this proposal and were persistent, and successful, in thwarting his licence application on many occasions. Finally, and with lots of assurances that it was going to be a brewery tap with real ale and not some rowdy lager lout pub with anti-social behaviour, he was finally allowed to open his doors to customers in 2007. It divides opinion, but those that like it really like it. It doesn't really feel like a pub, but it does have a certain something.

Again, there was good beer, a warm welcome and he ran a tight ship. He employed competent, smart, knowledgeable bar staff several of whom are still there many years later in varying capacities as he built his 'Team Steam.' It had a lively tea time crowd, even on the supposedly quiet nights earlier in the week. A dozen customers might not sound much, but there are plenty of small pubs that would kill to have a dozen customers in sinking a few pints each on a Monday teatime. Its success caused an expansion of the bar into what was the brewing area, doubling the size of the bar with brewing activity moved. It took something of its character away making it seem less cosy but the expanded tap does have its own merits.

Although there are pockets of revitalised pubs around Halifax town centre, much of it remains in a state of permanent decline. Some nice new micropubs are opening but the pubs of the past get more and more depressing and empty with the passage of time. A once vibrant pub scene that drew people from around the north of England is just a small selection of grotty pubs with ever dwindling footfall and an air of menace and unpleasantness. Even the Street Angels, volunteers who patrolled the streets on weekend evenings offering comfort to drunken revellers announced in 2012 that they were dropping their Friday night duty because there wasn't enough 'trade' for them.

With the exception of a few great new places such as the Alexandra Beerhouse, the Pumproom and the Grayston Unity, all small micropubs, there is more, and better, choice further afield. Leeds became a popular destination to explore for quiet midweek eating and drinking thanks to shift work. The ambitious Leeds Brewery is now Leeds' biggest brewery and has opened some fine pubs in the city centre. Its Brewery Tap, just around the corner from the train station, is all neutral colours and wooden floors with a good selection of their beers as well as other breweries though they are served at hefty prices.

Hipsters and entrepreneurs arrived, as well as the corporate chains, opening new and interesting places such as the North Bar and Tapped. Brewdog has its critics but I like it on a quiet afternoon once I have got over the prices. My favourite place is just a bit further down the road from the Leeds Brewery Tap and is the once tiny but now expanded Friends of Ham where interesting beers can be washed down with delicious platters of meats and cheeses. It was opened by trendy young exiles from London with a focus on quality drink and snacks and there is not a pickled egg in sight.

Much as I might hanker for those Tetley pubs of old, the only constant in life is change. Things come and go, places open and close, times change, fashions change and they will continue to do so. I hope the micropubs survive in Halifax and maybe that they even spur a renaissance to improve some of the badly neglected pubs that are in the town. People still want to go to pubs and spend money and these new places show that if they are done right, then people will come.

I've had a wonderful time with beer on both sides of the bar over the years and I hope it will continue. Will Friends of Ham be my next Big Six, still there in another twenty-five years and still doing what it does best? I hope so, just as I hope the Big Six will still be the special place it has been all these years. I have no idea what things will be like in another twenty-five years, but I do hope that I'm still able to prop up the bar to find out.

ABOUT THE AUTHOR

James Kirkham was born in Halifax, West Yorkshire in 1971. He currently lives and works in Abu Dhabi where he really misses proper beer.

https://wandojames.blogspot.com
https://www.facebook.com/jjk666
Twitter: @wandojames

22654994R00077

Printed in Great Britain
by Amazon